Florida's Snakes

Florida A&M University, Tallahassee
Florida Atlantic University, Boca Raton
Florida Gulf Coast University, Ft. Myers
Florida International University, Miami
Florida State University, Tallahassee
University of Central Florida, Orlando
University of Florida, Gainesville
University of North Florida, Jacksonville
University of South Florida, Tampa
University of West Florida, Pensacola

University Press of Florida

Gainesville Tallahassee Tampa Boca Raton Pensacola Orlando Miami Jacksonville Ft. Myers

# FLORIDA'S *Snakes*

## A Guide to Their Identification and Habits

R. D. Bartlett and Patricia Bartlett

Foreword by Carl D. May

08  07  06  05  04  03   6  5  4  3  2  1

All photos by R. D. Bartlett unless otherwise credited.

Library of Congress Cataloging-in-Publication Data
Bartlett, Richard D., 1938–
Florida's snakes: a guide to their identification and habits /
R. D. Bartlett and Patricia P. Bartlett; foreword by Carl D. May.
p. cm.
Includes bibliographical references (p. ).
ISBN 0-8130-2636-9 (pbk.: alk. paper)
1. Snakes—Florida—Identification. I. Bartlett, Patricia Pope, 1949–
II. Title.
QL666.O6B329 2003
597.96'09759—dc21      2003047337

The University Press of Florida is the scholarly publishing agency
for the State University System of Florida, comprising Florida A&M
University, Florida Atlantic University, Florida Gulf Coast University,
Florida International University, Florida State University, University
of Central Florida, University of Florida, University of North Florida,
University of South Florida, and University of West Florida.

University Press of Florida
15 Northwest 15th Street
Gainesville, FL 32611-2079
http://www.upf.com

# Contents

## NONVENOMOUS $\mathcal{S}nakes$

### Native Snakes

#### Colubrine Snakes; Typical or Colubrid Snakes, Family Colubridae   31

## Introduced and Peripheral Nonvenomous Snakes

## Peripheral Nonvenomous Snakes

# VENOMOUS *Snakes*

## Native Snakes

# Foreword

Florida has always been a paradise for reptiles. From one end of the state to the other, seemingly in every habitat, reptiles have flourished. But through the decades, Florida has changed. Humans have altered habitats, in many cases drastically. It is well documented that native plants and animals—snakes included—have suffered from these changes.

And yet the reptiles remain. While some species are perilously close to extinction, others are flourishing. Florida, it seems now, will continue to be the same paradise for reptiles as it is for humans. However, sooner or later the paths of humans and reptiles will cross. How humans react will in most cases be directly related to their understanding of the reptile in front of them. This is especially true when it comes to snakes (and the snakelike legless lizards), the most evocative grouping of Florida's reptiles.

Not all of Florida's changes have been adverse. Thanks to the immeasurable growth of the information highway, we have come in recent years to far better understand the role that snakes play in the environment, with the result that chance encounters with a reptile do not always result in its immediate and unceremonious killing.

We also now know that a specific kind of snake—a kingsnake, for example—may look very different in one part of Florida than it looks in another. To use another example, corn snakes—one of Florida's most beautiful species—are almost always studies in some shade of red, but their background colors can be dramatically different. These differing colors are called morphs.

We owe much of this current knowledge to people like Dick and Patti Bartlett. For most of the past three decades, they have undertaken the task of exploring Florida in order to become familiar not only with the state's reptiles but also with their habitats. For the Bartletts, it is not just a matter of knowing that a certain species may be found in a given area; they also know where in that area one would be most apt to find it. They have become intimately aware of the niche preferred by each species and subspecies. And wherever the Bartletts have traveled, Dick's cameras have gone too. It has been Dick's ambition to find and photograph all of Florida's snakes in natural habitats. This has been no small task. Some of our snakes are so secretive or rare that even when living in the heart of the range of a given species, many people are unaware that the snakes exist. The Bartletts have spent months, sometimes years, to finally find these snakes in the wild.

To the uninitiated, trying to identify a given snake can be confusing and frustrating. There are nonvenomous snakes that look very similar to venomous ones, and vice versa. *Florida's Snakes* helps both the long-time resident and the new arrival to our state identify and appreciate not only these wonderful reptiles but the look-alike legless lizards as well. With its superb photographs and easy to understand text, the Bartletts' field guide is like no other. It contains the means to know what a certain snake looks like, where it will be found, and much more. It also contains Dick and Patti Bartlett's enthusiasm for our wildlife heritage, and everyone will benefit from that.

Carl D. May

# Preface

Today most people will at least admit that snakes are interesting. This doesn't necessarily mean that everyone likes snakes, but interest is often the beginning of understanding. And snakes need understanding by the general public very badly, for of the reptiles, snakes are the most consistently persecuted. Almost everyone will tolerate—even enjoy—the presence of an anole or skink in their garden, but if that same person happens to turn up a small snake or a legless lizard (which is often mistaken for a snake), a miniwar is often declared. It is the legless creature that almost invariably comes out the loser.

Interest in these beleaguered reptiles often begins early in life—a human's life, not a snake's. Interpretive programs are often presented to kindergarteners. Enlightening programs may be offered periodically throughout the school years. Nature centers that often have live snakes on display and offer hands-on programs to audiences are now commonplace in many large cities. Pet stores offer snakes as pets. Herp expos (gigantic reptile shows), which seem to be held somewhere in the nation almost every weekend, bring together several hundred breeders and vendors of snakes and husbandry supplies and have walk-through observers and customers numbering in the thousands. Yes, folks are definitely becoming more interested in these legless reptiles, even if tolerance is somewhat slower in coming.

We had the privilege of first seeing snakes in the wild of Florida in the early 1950s, when most species were truly common. Sadly, in the ensuing years we have seen an undocumented but noticeable reduction in the numbers of virtually all. Many species are still common—at least by today's standards—but when compared with the vast numbers of yesteryear, we see that even these species actually are far less frequently encountered. Many factors, natural and otherwise (but mostly otherwise), have taken a toll. Attribute the lessened numbers to decades of persecution, habitat fragmentation, and the resulting death of migrating snakes by vehicles (yes, indeed, snakes do make minimigrations!); to collection from the wild for one or another purposes; and most recently to the (again undocumented) predation by imported fire ants. Perhaps the surprise should be not that Florida's snakes are reduced in numbers but that they continue to exist at all.

Florida has about eighty recognizable species, subspecies, and color morphs of snakes within its boundaries. Most of these are native; a few are introduced. Within these pages we offer pictures of and information on all, as well as on five legless lizards that are often mistaken for snakes.

We invite you to join us in a tour of the habitats and snake species you may encounter in the Sunshine State.

## Acknowledgments

Thanks are due many people for many types of contributions.

Over a span of five decades, field companions have varied. Friends like Gordy Johnston, Dennie Miller, Ralph Curtis, John Truitt, Dade Thornton, Dennis Cathcart, Kenny Wray, Tom Tyning, John Lewis, Regis Opferman, Paul Moler, Billy Griswold, Walter Meshaka, Flavio Morrisey, Rob MacInnes, Barry Mansell, Carl May, Kevin Zippel, Scott Cushnir, Chris Bednarski, Mike Manfredi, Frank Weed, Louie Porras, Rhea Warren, and Wayne Van Devender have done much to make enjoyable interludes in the field even more so.

Ron Sayers was not only a great field companion but an equally great photography teacher.

John Decker has been a tutor in the lore and habits of the Keys herpetofauna; he also provided some rarely seen snakes for photographs. Mark Robertson and Rob Ferran have done likewise with North Florida species. David Auth allowed us to photograph a preserved specimen (there are no live ones known) of Florida's least-familiar snake, the South Florida rainbow snake.

Time and again, Bill Love and Rob MacInnes have provided us with opportunities to photograph needed specimens.

Dan Pearson steered us toward photographers such as Jim Duquesnel, who graciously provided us with comments about and pictures of Florida Keys coral snakes and their food snake, the very rare rim rock crowned snake. Bruce Morgan showed us the most unusual and spectacular Keys-phase yellow rat snake that we have ever seen and shared tales of a Florida long gone. Robert Tregembo introduced us to the South Florida mole kingsnake, a rare creature that he sought eagerly and with which he became very familiar.

To these folks, and to all others who have offered field assistance and comments over the years, we extend our sincerest appreciation.

**Introduction**

The automobile was built at a price that travelers could afford, and the travelers came—to Florida.

Continents and oceans were crossed first by slow airplanes propelled by giant propellers, then by fast airplanes propelled by jet engines, and the travelers came—to Florida.

Buses and trains brought others; some came on ships, some in tiny power boats, but come they did—to Florida.

Some came and left, thought a while, and returned to stay. Some, once here, never again left the state. Travelers no more, they were now residents—of Florida.

As residents arrived, enthralled by a moderate to balmy climate, by vast beaches, and by an acceptable cost of living, Florida's wild spaces diminished. And as wild Florida receded, into its wake came railroads, roads, airports, and malls. Singly these changes meant little. Combined, they made a vast difference.

Gone is most of the Everglades—that vast sea of sawgrass that once waved from and shaded shallow, slowly flowing waters stretching from the Kissimmee Prairie north of Lake Okeechobee to Flamingo at the southernmost tip of the mainland. Gone are the pristine rivers. Gone is the biodiversity of the Fakahatchee Strand. But, although they are present in lesser numbers, some things—including much of our wildlife—remain. Some are threatened or endangered, all are hemmed in by increasingly fragmented habitats, and a few are now battling with competing introduced alien species.

Either favorably or adversely, Florida's snakes have long fascinated Florida's human population. Snakes have suffered from bad press, and only today is a fear and loathing of these intriguing and immensely beneficial reptiles slowly being replaced by tolerance and understanding. Misconceptions were and still are prevalent, however. Some snakes might have benefited from misunderstandings. Because kingsnakes and indigo snakes (the "blue bull snakes" of rural Floridians) were thought to be the diehard enemies of other snakes—including the venomous forms—they were tolerated. The truth is that when they are hungry these big harmless snakes certainly do eat venomous and other snakes, but they *don't* kill every other snake in their vicinity, and they *do* eat many other animals besides. Conversely, the harmless little scarlet ("coral") kingsnake and the lizard-egg-eating scarlet snake have suffered at the hands of humans because of their similarity in appearance to the venomous eastern coral snake.

Are there more misconceptions and myths? Indeed, there are many, and we try to dispel all in the appropriate species accounts. In these pages we have discussed all forty-four species (seventy-four subspecies, intergrades, and color variants) of Florida's native snakes. This includes three kinds that are introduced and breeding in the state, three that are introduced but not yet known to be breeding, and six whose ranges come right to the Florida state line in either Alabama or Georgia. We have included the five species of legless reptiles that are often mistaken for snakes. This coverage will allow you to identify any native Florida species and most introduced forms, and it should prevent confusion if you happen to take a few steps into one of our neighboring states.

We hope you'll enjoy learning more about these interesting creatures, part of Florida's natural, yet altered, ecosystem.

**Florida Habitats**

Balmy subtropical winters or those with a surprising chill—which of these you experience will depend on where in Florida you are. At a latitude of about 24.5 degrees north, with temperatures stabilized and moderated by the surrounding waters, Key West can consistently offer some of the most desirable temperatures to be found in the United States. Winter lows are seldom less than 60°F and are often at least five degrees higher. Miami—150 miles to the northeast of Key West—has water on only one side and therefore lacks the temperature stability of the Keys. It can be somewhat cooler in the winter (but often isn't) and warmer in the summer (and often is). Conversely, Floridians along the Georgia and Alabama state lines (approximate latitude of 31 degrees) periodically sport an interesting array of winter clothing and do their share of shivering each winter as well.

The snakes at the southern end of the state—like the people—seldom undergo winter dormancy because of the cold. It is in the Miami area that so many tropical alien pet-trade species have become established. Snake activity is more seasonal in Florida's north. During the times that the human population is donning its cumbersome and often gaudy winter livery, the snake fauna is quiescent—undergoing a period of winter dormancy in areas of seclusion known best only to themselves.

Not only does it have a diverse climate, but for a flat state—a *very* flat state (the highest point is only some 350 feet above sea level)—Florida has a surprising number of very diverse habitats. There are three divisions each of xeric (dry) habitats and mesic (damp) habitats. Add to these four described types of hydric (periodically wet) flatlands habitats, two types of limestone communities, plus several divisions each of disturbed habitats, aquatic habitats, and dune-beach communities.

As might be expected, average temperatures and habitat diversity contribute prominently to the diversity of Florida's snake fauna.

## Habitats and Inhabitants Defined

*Xeric* habitats are well-drained, usually upland (ridge) areas with few permanent water sources. Cacti, wiregrass, lichens, longleaf pines, sand pines, several species of oaks, and saw palmettos are among the plants found in these regions. The subdesignations often used within xeric habitats are scrub, sandhills, and upland hammocks. Fire plays an important role in maintaining these sometimes transient habitats, inhibiting their natural succession by other habitats. Snakes such as diamond-backed rattlers, coral snakes, scarlet snakes, pine snakes, racers, coachwhips, and crowned snakes inhabit these areas.

*Mesic* designations include damp upland, flatland, and prairie habitats that often have water sources such as permanent or temporary ponds or creeks. Trees such as holly, beeches, magnolias, and spruce pines grow profusely in the upland regions. Longleaf pines are also found in the flatwoods. Flatwoods usually have a sparse understory, but herbaceous plants from catsclaw to composites vie for supremacy on the wet prairies. Palmettos and willows are the commonly seen prairie trees. Brown snakes, garter snakes, racers, rat snakes, kingsnakes, and rattlesnakes are among the snake species commonly encountered in such habitats.

*Hydric* describes habitats that vary from the well-known and beleaguered Everglades to wet prairies, cypress heads, and river swamps. In other words, these habitats are often (some perpetually) wet. Water snakes, garter snakes, green snakes, racers, rat snakes, cottonmouths, and pygmy rattlesnakes are some of the snake inhabitants.

*Limestone* habitats are restricted to South Florida, including the Keys. Mahogany, poisonwood, paurotis and sabal palms, slash pines, and a hostile (to humans) hodgepodge of understory plants are present. Expect to see corn snakes, pygmy rattlers, racers, ring-necked snakes, and ribbon snakes here.

Disturbed habitats—residences, road verges (including the trees planted there), pastures, and trash piles among them—are home to many of the more adaptable snakes. Among others, you may see rat snakes, kingsnakes, pine woods snakes, earth snakes, brown snakes, and pygmy rattlesnakes.

Coastal dunes and the adjacent beaches—with or without sea oats, bindweed, railroad vine, and tiny oaks—may be populated by some of the crowned snakes and ring-necked snakes and visited occasionally by racers and garter snakes.

Freshwater and marine habitats may be divided into two groups. Ephemeral ponds, permanent ponds and lakes, canals, creeks, rivers, and freshwater marshes comprise one grouping. Salt marshes, mangrove swamps, and the open ocean are the second. Although some snakes—diamond-backed rattlesnakes, for example—may occasionally cross stretches of salt water, in Florida there is no snake that swims regularly in the open ocean, and only the three races of salt marsh snake are adapted to mangrove and salt marsh habitats.

On the other hand, freshwater habitats are among the most heavily populated of Florida's habitats, housing all manner of water snakes, cottonmouths, ribbon snakes, swamp snakes, crayfish snakes, mud snakes, and rainbow snakes.

# How to Use This Book

There are many ways to format a field guide, and each provides its own set of problems for a user. We have simply listed species first by family and subfamily, then alphabetically by scientific name. An accepted common name has also been provided. Photographs of every type discussed, including color variations, have been provided. We have issued a number to each species, subspecies, or variant. The same number applies both for picture and discussion (for example, both the species account and the photo of the corn snake are number 15, while the discussion and photo of the color variant from the Lower Keys are number 16).

If you are reasonably sure of what kind of snake you are looking at, begin your search in the table of contents or the index. If you have no idea, begin your search in the photo section and proceed from there to the text and the range maps. Remember, though, that range maps are inherently inaccurate. This is especially true today, when large numbers of snakes are collected from the wild or are captive bred for the pet trade and may escape or be released far from their normal range. (For examples, see the section on introduced exotic snakes beginning on page 130. None of these should be in Florida, but all—some in self-sustaining breeding populations—are definitely here.) Range maps should be considered a crutch—definitely not the final word—in snake identification.

Also consider habitats when attempting identification. Although snakes may occasionally be very much out of place, do not expect to find a swamp snake in high, dry sandhills habitat nor a crowned snake sunning in a river-edge shrub.

For example, say that you are canoeing along a central peninsula waterway, and you see a dark, heavy-bodied snake lying on some sunlit willow branches that overhang the water. Water snake? Cottonmouth? One's venomous, and one's not, but which is it? By now, your craft is drifting quietly along with the current (take care that the boat does not get positioned so the snake can drop into it if startled), and you have opened to the grouping of water snakes in the photo section. The snake is big—probably 4 feet long—a dark olive (maybe with vague darker bands), and you can see its face and chin are yellowish. It has no well-defined markings on its face, and the scales are rough. You can see that the belly is light and doesn't seem to have any definitive markings.

Thumbing through the water snake plates, you home in on either the Florida green water snake or the Mississippi green water snake. Both are nonvenomous. But could it be a cottonmouth? You certainly don't want to make a mistake. You flip to the cottonmouth photo in the venomous section and see that although the color is almost right, the cottonmouth has a strong and distinctive facial pattern. Mystery **almost** solved. You know it's not a cottonmouth. But which of the green water snakes is it? The photo of the Mississippi green water snake shows a patterned belly; that pretty much rules out that species. Your identification is confirmed when you turn to the text to double-check your identification. Range maps show that the Mississippi green water snake does not occur in Central Florida. Description, habitat, and range map of the Florida green water snake all check out. At about that time, your canoe brushes the branch, and with a start, the big snake plunges into the water. Habits—fleeing, not fighting—now check out also. It's early in the day, you've already seen a Florida green water snake, and there's a lot of river yet before you. You've made a good beginning!

# Captive Care

A Cursory Compilation

---

Captive care information in a field guide?

Although we do not advocate the collecting of any wildlife for commercial purposes, we do strongly believe that any person interested in keeping a non-restricted reptile or amphibian should be able to do so. Having accurate husbandry information immediately available may ease the transition for the snake. Not all of Florida's snake species are equally easy to keep, nor are all of equal interest to most observers. (Most interest has always been shown in the nonregulated constricting lampropeltines, then to a lesser degree in garter snakes, hog-noses, and last, the venomous species. To keep the venomous or restricted species, you must have a permit from the Florida Fish and Wildlife Conservation Commission. If the snake is federally protected, a permit from the Department of the Interior's Fish and Wildlife Service will be needed.)

We do not delve deeply into captive care but have included the basics in each family account. There are a great many books available that provide detailed husbandry information. But the husbandry basics are pretty standard:

1. Dry, clean, *escape-proof* caging *of suitable size.* Suitable size can be calculated several ways. One matches the gallonage with the inch length. A ten-inch snake needs a ten-gallon tank; a thirty-inch snake needs a thirty-gallon tank. In brief, a twenty-gallon to 30-gallon tank is large enough for most Florida snakes, up to six feet in length. Snakes are escape artists par excellence. Choose the caging wisely. In most cases, an aquarium will suffice nicely, and clip-on tops are readily available at pet stores.
2. Suitable substrate. This may be clean newspapers, nonbleached paper towels, aspen shavings, or, for burrowing species, clean sand of the type in which they were found. We recommend against using the sharp-grained silica play sand available at home improvement stores. If the substrate is dirty or too wet (or especially dirty *and* too wet),

the snakes in that cage will often develop unsightly, difficult to cure, and sometimes lethal skin disorders.

3. Suitable cage temperature. This is somewhat variable by species, but try to provide a thermal gradient. A temperature of 82 to 90°F on one end of the cage and not lower than 70°F on the other, cool end is usually fine.

4. A water container, always with fresh water. The relative size of this may vary by species. A sand-dune-dwelling species can be kept with only a small amount of water, while a species that immerses itself to soak periodically will need a greater amount of water.

5. A hide box. Snakes thrive best when they feel secure.

6. Suitable food—both in type and in quantity—readily available. We urge that you feed your snake prekilled prey. If you can't get your snake to feed within a reasonable period of time (from four to six weeks), it should be released exactly where it was found. If captive bred, a snake should *never* be released. Not only will it muddy up the local gene pool for that species, but your snake has no established territory and may not be able to establish one. Since snakes are ecto-thermic (cold-blooded) creatures, the ability to remain in prime health is directly related to the continuous availability of fresh water in their cage and to the cage temperature. Even when warm cage tempera-tures are maintained, the appetite of many snakes will diminish (or may shut down entirely) in the winter.

In addition to books, at least three excellent additional sources of hus-bandry information exist. These are herp expos, herpetological societies, and the Internet. Herp expos are essentially gigantic indoor yard sales of reptiles, amphibians, and support equipment. They are held periodically in many of the larger cities in the United States, Canada, and Europe. Herpetological so-cieties also exist in many of the larger cities. Information on nearby herpeto-logical societies can be obtained from pet stores, museums, or similar sources. The Internet, at myriad websites, provides interactive chat rooms, forums, and information on many common and rare species.

Many captive snakes are easily cared for and housed. This is especially true of the rat snakes and kingsnakes, the water snakes, the garter snakes, and the hog-nosed snakes. The fully aquatic forms—among them the crayfish snakes, swamp snakes, mud snakes, and rainbow snakes—are very difficult to keep and should not be collected. Several of Florida's tiny burrowing species are difficult to feed and do not make particularly good terrarium candidates.

Most snakes do not seem to need full-spectrum lighting, and many species will accept prekilled prey. Many snakes require feeding only once a week, and some need it even less often.

When planning a caging setup, do not be deceived by a snake's name. For example, although they are called water snakes, the semiaquatic species in the genus *Nerodia* will quickly develop potentially fatal skin lesions if they are kept perpetually wet.

Today, commercial reptile cages of many shapes and sizes are available to hobbyists. It is no longer necessary to convert aquaria into terraria, although it is certainly perfectly acceptable to do so. No matter the source of your caging, be certain that the terrarium/cage is tightly covered.

Provide your snake with suitable cage furniture—climbing limbs, an easily cleaned substrate, and a hiding box are a good start. The very slender and almost feather-light rough green snake is at home in twig-tip foliage, but even it prefers the stability offered by vine tangles. Perches or limbs should be a minimum of one-and-a-half times the diameter of the snake's body. By nature, snakes are secretive beasts, but some hide more persistently than others, especially during the daylight hours. Snakes always do best as captives when they feel safe and secure. Although perfectly hardy, the scarlet kingsnake is one of the most secretive of all snakes. This species will probably spend most of its time beneath the substrate. The larger kingsnakes do much the same. Pine snakes, corn snakes, rat snakes, garter snakes, and ribbon snakes will prefer a hide box that is barely big enough for them to coil within.

Snakes are ectothermic creatures that regulate their body temperatures by utilizing outside sources of heating and cooling. At most times they warm by choosing a secluded place and basking in the sun. Prior to skin shedding—when their eyes are "blue" and vision is impaired—they are more secretive, seeking warmth beneath ground-surface litter. Provide your snake the ability to thermoregulate in its cage. This may be accomplished with undertank heaters or with overhead lights. Because hot-rocks have malfunctioned and burned snakes using them, we do not recommend them.

Florida snakes may become semidormant during the short days of winter, even if their cage temperature is maintained suitably warm. At this time they may also refuse food.

Naturally changing weather patterns—dry seasons, rainy seasons, low-pressure frontal systems, the high pressure associated with fine weather, even the lunar cycle—are known to affect snake behavior. Many nocturnal snakes are most active during the dark of the moon or during unsettled weather. Reproductive behavior is often stimulated by the elevated humidity and lowering barometric pressures that occur before a storm.

If your snake is "opaque" or "blue"—the condition assumed prior to skin-shedding when the snake's eyes actually take on a blue or cloudy coloration—you may wish to have a water dish, large enough to allow your snake to soak, in the cage.

Despite being carnivorous, snakes exhibit all degrees of dietary specialization. Some undergo age-related changes in diet preferences. Rat snakes are among these. In the wild, the hatchlings of many rat snakes eat lizards and frogs (especially tree frogs), but with increasing age they become efficient hunters and prefer to prey on rodents (and birds). For a captive snake to eat properly, you must offer it the correct type of food in a setting the snake finds secure.

There are two things that you can do if your snake is a temperate species and a winter nonfeeder. You can cool the animal into a state of dormancy, or you can fuss with it—changing lighting, warmth, and feeding parameters—and hope that you hit on the combination that induces the snake to feed before the lengthening daylight hours of springtime automatically do so. In most cases, the cooling is the easier of the two. If your snake is one of those that stops eating seasonally, it is imperative that it be at optimum weight (a little on the heavy side of normal) as autumn approaches.

There is a growing body of evidence to suggest that what is a natural diet for a snake is the best diet in captivity. Although in the wild many snakes (such as rat snakes) eat a diet consisting of primarily one type of prey, others (such as kingsnakes) are entirely opportunistic in feeding preferences. Humans have a tendency to feed all snakes the prey items most easily obtained, if the snake will eat that prey. Thus, we strive to adapt eastern hog-nosed snakes—that feed upon toads in the wild—to a diet of mice, and we feed indigo snakes, a species with a very catholic diet, only rats. On such diets, indigo snakes often refuse to breed, and eastern hog-noses seem to have a shortened life span.

# How and Where to Find Snakes

Finding a snake is often very much a matter of luck (either good or bad, depending on how you happen to feel about these creatures). Even with what we like to think of as a degree of expertise in knowing the habits of snakes, we sometimes have looked long and hard and failed dismally in our search. At other times, we have found an unsuspected species in an unsuspected place at very unsuspected times.

For example, we have lived in our Gainesville, Florida, house for a number of years. We have a large yard in which we know a number of snake species exist. One day, wishing to upgrade our photos of a Central Florida crowned snake, I walked back to a large board under which we had almost always found one or more for the last several years. But this time, the overturned board revealed not crowned snakes but rather two pine woods snakes, which we had never seen there before. Where had the pine woods snakes been on previous occasions? We just don't know. Nor do we understand why they remained beneath that board for several weeks and then disappeared, not to be seen again. Once again when we turn the board to find a snake, it is almost always a crowned snake.

Ten other snake species can be seen rather regularly in our yard and are expected. The eleventh, the eastern diamond-backed rattlesnake, was unexpected (but appreciated nonetheless).

When you are hoping to find a snake of a given species, careful attention must be given to its habitat preferences, to its range, and to its activity patterns. If you wish to find a green water snake, you would go to a pond, wet prairie, or river, not to the elevated, sandy Lake Wales ridge. If it is a Mississippi green water snake you hope to see, you sure wouldn't head for Central or South Florida, where the Florida green water snake holds court. Rather, you'd head for the western panhandle, knowing all the while that because of its extremely limited range in Florida, you would probably fail in your quest.

Using the same logic, you probably won't see a Florida pine snake in dank woodlands with clay-type soils, or a Gulf salt marsh snake in a freshwater marsh in eastern Florida. But a black racer? That's a different story. Racers tolerate and occupy a wide variety of habitats and may be found almost throughout the state. But they are diurnal in their activity patterns. Come nightfall, every self-respecting racer will find a hiding place for the night and will remain there until the next morning's sun begins rewarming the earth.

Florida and eastern kingsnakes are also *usually* primarily diurnal in their activity patterns, but on warm spring or summer evenings they may remain active until well after dark. Conversely, their little congener, the scarlet kingsnake, is seldom surface-active by day but may be found crossing roadways or trails on warm to hot spring and summer nights—especially if a pending storm is lowering barometric pressure.

At the same time that scarlet kingsnakes are active, scarlet snakes are too.

With only a half-dozen exceptions, every eastern coral snake we have ever seen has been surface-active by day or in the early dusk. With only two exceptions, every encounter we have had with a diamond-backed rattlesnake has been during the day. One exception was a rattler found crossing a roadway at midnight during a blinding rainstorm that interrupted a lengthy drought.

Conversely, we have found both the dusky pygmy rattlesnake and the canebrake phase of the timber rattlesnake active and moving far more often in the gathering dusk or after dark than in the hours of daylight.

Water snakes, crayfish snakes, swamp snakes, and mud snakes often emerge from their muddy lairs and come into the shallows after darkness has fallen. Then they can be easily seen with the aid of a flashlight. On some spring and early summer nights, these snakes may indulge in mass movements that seem almost like migrations, leaving their home waters seemingly in search of new and fresh territories (or, since this is the breeding season, are they searching for or following pheromone trails in search of a receptive mate?). Whichever the reason, there are times when vehicles kill dozens or even hundreds of these natricines trying to cross busy roadways. In fact, many snakes, both common and rare, are found by researchers and hobbyists driving at night. Watching for crossing snakes in the glare of your headlamps can be a dangerous preoccupation that is illegal in some areas. Accidents and even fatalities have occurred.

Snakes are apt to be encountered any place and any time in Florida. But with a little research you can enhance your chances of meeting—or avoiding—these interesting and often secretive reptiles.

# About Snakes

## Prey and Prey Procurement

Despite having no limbs and relatively poor hearing, snakes are amazingly proficient in finding and overcoming prey. Plainly stated, snakes are eminently efficient predators. In searching for prey, some snakes burrow, some climb, many swim, some actively pursue prey, while others are wait-and-ambush hunters, positioning themselves next to trails used by their favored prey animals. How is all of this accomplished? Why are snakes so successful? How do they know where game trails are? How can a pit viper strike unerringly in absolute darkness?

The answers to these questions are pretty straightforward. Although a few snakes find their prey by sight, most, if not all, are far more dependent on olfactory senses than on sight. In fact, scent leads snakes not only to prey but to receptive mates as well.

But snakes smell their prey with their tongue. Contrary to one popular belief, the tongue of a snake cannot inflict injury of any kind. Rather, while extended—forked tips usually parted—the tongue of a snake gathers information. Scent particles are picked up, and when the tongue is withdrawn, the particles are brought into contact with and analyzed by the very sensitive Jacobson's organ in the palate. Once identified, the object can be either sought (its scent trail followed) or avoided. Most snakes require visual stimulation to trigger a strike.

In Florida, there are only a few snakes that rely on visual cues when hunting. Primary among these are the racers, the coachwhip, and the indigo snake. When hunting, all of these snake species will glide swiftly along, then raise their head well above the surrounding vegetation—in an action called periscoping—in an apparent effort to see a prey animal in motion. The hop of a frog or an unusual waving of the grass will cause these active snakes to alter paths and search earnestly for the potential prey animal. Once on the trail, these snakes use both sight and scent to track and catch the prey.

Snakes that primarily utilize a wait-and-ambush strategy may depend on visual cues as a secondary method of finding prey. A rat snake, rattlesnake, or green snake may be alerted by the movement of a potential prey animal, but the snake's ultimate course is largely determined by scent.

Some snakes carry the wait-and-ambush strategy a step further. They actually lure prey to their location. The young of some rather inactive snakes (copperheads and cottonmouths) have a contrastingly colored tail tip. To lure their prey, the coiled snake elevates and writhes the tail tip above the coils and near its head. A frog or lizard, seeing what it thinks is a succulent caterpillar, approaches and itself becomes a prey item.

As a group Florida snakes exhibit all degrees of dietary generalization. For example, kingsnakes and the indigo snake eat nearly anything they can overpower. There are insect eaters (rough green snake), worm eaters (garter snakes and brown snakes), fish eaters (ribbon snakes and water snakes), and toad eaters (eastern hog-nosed snakes). There are eaters of frogs and lizards (racers and coachwhips), slug eaters (red-bellied snakes), and many that feed on birds and mammals (rat snakes and pine snakes).

A hungry snake is more alert and active than a sated one. Many Florida snake species hunt and feed diurnally (racers, indigo snakes, green snakes, hog-nosed snakes, some kingsnakes, pine snakes), but others, such as the rat snake, hunt nocturnally. Probably most species are opportunistic hunters, feeding whenever they encounter an appropriate prey animal.

Snakes overpower their prey in several ways. Some simply seize a small food animal and immediately begin swallowing. A larger prey animal, once grasped, may be partially immobilized by a loop of the snake's body simply holding it to the ground. Racers and indigo snakes use this method. Other snake species—such as the pine snakes, rat snakes, and kingsnakes—are powerful constrictors that kill their prey in powerful, ever-tightening coils before eating it. No bones are broken during constriction. The coils simply tighten until the prey can no longer breathe. And, of course, we all know about prey procurement by envenomation, a method used by the coral snake and pit vipers.

Even in Florida—especially in the more temperate parts of the state—many snakes reduce their feeding or may cease to eat entirely during the cool months of the year. Some species become inactive, at least during a cold front; some may actually hibernate (brumate) through the winter months. In South Florida, where temperatures are basically benign year around, lowered humidity, slightly cooler nighttime temperatures, and fewer hours of daylight provide snakes their seasonal cues and cause hormonal changes that reduce the urge to feed but prepare the snakes for breeding.

Some snakes fast during their breeding season, and females may not feed for several days or weeks prior to egg or clutch deposition.

## Snake reproduction

The breeding biology of snakes is quite dissimilar to that of other classes of vertebrates. Such phenomena as sperm retention (sometimes for a period of years), weather and photoperiod stimulation, and varying modes of birth are well documented in snakes.

Male snakes have dual reproductive organs termed hemipenes. Only a single hemipene is used during each incidence of copulation. The breeding activities of snakes seem to be dictated by both external and internal phenomena. Breeding most often occurs in spring, but it also may occur in autumn. External stimuli such as rapidly dropping barometric pressure or a sustained low-pressure system often induce breeding activities. Reproductively receptive females produce pheromones that further excite the males and permit them to trail her. Courtship is minimal. When receptive, the female will often elevate her tail. Breeding is rather simple, with the male lying next to, or arced across, the body of the female; often their tails are entwined. Cloacae are juxtaposed, allowing intromission of one of the male's hemipenes. Copulation may last from a few minutes to many hours. When they are healthy and food is ample, females of some egg-laying species are known to lay twice or even three times (to double- or triple-clutch) in a season. Clutches are usually laid 3½ to 4½ weeks apart. Subsequent clutches are often smaller than the first. Egg viability may also be greatest in the first clutch of each season.

Because of the extended gestation duration, live-bearing snakes in Florida usually have only a single clutch each season. When conditions are adverse, females may produce a clutch only every second, third, or fourth year.

Sperm retention may allow a female to produce viable clutches for two or

## Table 1. Egg-laying vs. Live-bearing

| Egg-laying (oviparous) genera | Live-bearing (ovoviviparous) genera |
|---|---|
| Indigo snake | Elephant-trunk snake |
| Racers | Earth snakes |
| Coachwhips | Garter snakes and Ribbon snakes |
| Ring-necked snakes* | Water snakes and Salt marsh snakes |
| Worm snakes | Swamp snakes |
| Kingsnakes and Milksnakes | Crayfish snakes |
| Rat snakes and Corn snakes | Brown snakes and Red-bellied snakes |
| Pine snakes | Copperhead and Cottonmouths |
| Scarlet snakes | Rattlesnakes |
| Short-tailed snakes | |
| Hog-nosed snakes | |
| Crowned snakes | |
| Brahminy blind snake** | |
| Rough green snake | |
| Pine woods snake | |
| Mud snakes and Rainbow snakes | |
| Coral snake | |

* Although ring-necked snakes are normally oviparous, at least one incidence of viviparity has been documented.
** The Brahminy blind snake is an all-female, parthenogenic snake species. Although usually oviparous, an occasional incident of viviparity has been documented.

three years following a single mating. Small snake species may produce only 2 or 3 eggs or babies in each clutch. Larger species may produce 12 to 40 eggs or young. Occasionally immense clutches are produced. For example, female eastern garter snakes may have up to 60 babies in a clutch, and Florida green water snakes have been documented as having produced more than 120 young. The eggs of a large female eastern mud snake may number between 60 and 104 in a single clutch.

Snakes are ectothermic, depending on external stimuli to regulate bodily functions including gestation. Thermoregulation—basking in the warming rays of the sun or beneath a sun-warmed object—permits a snake to attain optimum body temperature. Gestation may last for 30 to 40 days (most egg-laying species) to well over 90 days (live-bearing species). Seriously adverse body temperatures (either too hot or too cold) may result in inviable eggs. Once eggs are laid, they too are dependent on suitable temperatures for successful incubation. Female snakes choose their egg-deposition site rather carefully, looking for a site that will retain a temperature of 80 to 85°F over most of each 24-hour period. (Gravid females of live-bearing species also thermoregulate carefully and extensively.) Although typically eggs may hatch after 45 to 65 days of incubation, if nest temperatures are overly warm (but not lethal), eggs may hatch in a shorter time; if nest temperatures are cooler, they may take longer. As with adverse temperatures during gestation, adverse temperatures during incubation can result in embryo deformities or death.

Hatchling or neonate snakes may look dramatically different from the adults. Also, the diet of a newly hatched or newly born snake may be quite different from that of an adult of the same species.

## Venom and Envenomation

Some snakes typically thought of as harmless utilize weak venoms to help them overcome their prey. A well-known and highly respected toxicologist, the late Sherman A. Minton, once asked, "Is there any such thing as a truly nonvenomous snake?"

Our answer to that query is, "We think so, but we're not entirely sure." The saliva of the lampropeltine colubrids (rat snakes, kingsnakes, and relatives), for example, *seems* to be devoid of toxins. So too do the salivas of many colubrine colubrids.

Certainly, though, a great many snakes—big and small—routinely designated as harmless or nonvenomous do produce a venom of sorts. In many cases, the venom seems to be rather species specific, meaning that it is more efficient in overcoming one kind of prey animal than another. For example, while the toxins contained in the saliva of the hog-nosed snake will quickly overcome a toad, they are less effective against endothermic (warm-blooded) prey such as a mouse and seem to do little more than cause localized lividity and edema in humans. Garter snakes and water snakes also produce salivary enzymes that produce a slight toxicity.

The phenomenon of toxicity in many of the so-called harmless snakes is not well understood. Some of these snakes seem considerably less harmless than others. For example, the bite of one of the Asian keelbacks—a natricine relative of the garter and the water snakes—has caused human death. With this in mind, although there has never even been a case of sickness attributed to any New World natricine, we must urge that caution be used when any are handled.

The salivary enzymes are produced in the Duvernoy's gland, a gland known to produce toxins of variable efficacy in rear-fanged snakes.

The rear teeth of many colubrid snakes, hog-noses among them, are greatly elongated and seem to have evolved primarily for producing wounds that allow entry into the prey of the enzyme-carrying saliva. These are, in effect, rear fangs. Fangs of this type have evolved separately in colubrid snakes of many subfamilies.

In America, the front-fanged snakes are the most dangerous. These snakes are contained in two families, the elapines (coral snakes) and the viperines (pit vipers). Restricting the discussion to Floridian snakes, the eastern coral snake has short, rigidly set (nonmovable) tubular fangs that deliver a neuro-toxic venom that is particularly efficient in killing its prey of snakes and lizards. Coral snakes are incapable of lunging strikes, instead biting and holding the victim.

The viperines—which include the copperhead, cottonmouths, and rattle-snakes—have long fangs affixed to a movable maxillary bone. These snakes produce venoms of variable compositions, but most are primarily haemo-toxic, effectively destroying blood cells, vessel walls, and blood-clotting mechanisms. The venom is usually delivered in a lunging strike, but these snakes are fully capable of administering a typical bite. Because the temperature sensitivity of the pits is so critically attuned, slight differences in one side from the other—even from so tiny a source as an approaching rodent—allow the snake to determine prey (or predator) position and strike almost unerringly, even in total darkness. Although the venom produced by all Florida pit vipers is typically and dangerously haemotoxic, the venom of the timber (canebrake) rattler in Florida also contains potent neurotoxins and is particularly dangerous. Insects, frogs, lizards, and small mammals are the chosen prey of the copperhead and the pygmy rattlesnake. Add fish to that list and you have the diet of the cottonmouth. The eastern diamond-back prefers rabbits but will accept other mammals and quail, and the timber rattlesnake eats birds, squirrels, rats, and rabbits. After being struck and envenomated, the prey of a pit viper dashes away but is usually quickly overcome by the venom. The pit viper then follows the scent trail left by the stricken prey animal. The venom not only kills the prey but acts upon the prey as a predigestant, destroying cell and vessel walls. Although all snakes are capable of eating proportionately large meals, animals consumed by pit vipers are often proportionately huge.

### Human Envenomation

Occasionally tables turn, and rather than human killing venomous snake, venomous snake bites human. In all fairness to the snake, most bites seem to occur while a human is attempting to kill or molest the snake or accidentally steps on the snake. The latter is not as hard to do as it may sound, for venomous snakes blend remarkably well with their background, even when cover is sparse.

Because snakes are able to regulate their venom output, not all bites from a venomous snake result in an actual envenomation. In fact, a good percentage of the bites ascertained to have been delivered by a venomous snake are "dry" bites—bites where the snake administered no venom. Other bites range from mild to moderate or full envenomations. The southern copperhead has a comparatively innocuous venom—not one you can overlook, mind you (the pain will soon have you wondering why you were careless enough to get bitten), but one that is not likely to be lethal. Neither is the dusky pygmy rattlesnake apt to deliver a lethal bite, because—despite a rather high drop-for-drop potency—the snake's small head makes the venom yield small. Again, it is not a bite that you will be able to ignore, but it is of less consequence than a bite from a cottonmouth or a larger species of rattlesnake. The cottonmouth can become very large and has a high output of quite toxic venom, but unless its victim is a tiny child or someone in poor overall health, the envenomation is not apt to be fatal. It will be very painful, tissue damage can be extreme, and—because cottonmouths are inveterate scavengers—the possibility of serious secondary infection must be routinely considered. A bite from a large eastern diamond-back or a large timber (canebrake) rattlesnake—especially a timber rattler from Florida—can be very serious. Your doctor may not be aware of the very high content of neurotoxins in timber rattlesnake venom and *must* be apprised. Envenomation by a large coral snake—another species with a large output of neurotoxins—is also very serious. Medical assessment is mandatory, and medical intervention is likely to be necessary.

Because of current controversies over the proper methods of treating a venomous snakebite, and because no two people react the same to the enzymes, peptides, and polypeptides of which snake venom largely consists, we refrain from delving into the medical techniques. We would urge, however, that if you seek venomous snakes in the field; are afield in areas where venomous snakes may be; keep venomous snakes in captivity; or are otherwise involved with these reptiles, you find a qualified doctor (who will use a conservative treatment approach) *before* a need arises. Antivenin for pit-viper bites, though very expensive, is readily available. It is far more difficult to obtain coral snake antivenin. Do keep in mind that reaction to the antivenin (a horse-serum derivative) can be as bad or, in some cases, worse than the actual envenomation. Medical treatment for the allergic reaction to the antivenin is often required.

# Snakes and the Florida Law

Florida laws or regulations address snakes in many ways. Some laws protect them, some regulations regulate captive conditions (caging requirements are precise), and other regulations pertain to the selling of snakes. A very specific set of regulations deals with the collecting and keeping of venomous snakes. You can obtain copies of all state regulations pertaining to the collecting, caging, and selling of snakes from:

State of Florida Fish and Wildlife Conservation Commission
620 South Meridian Street
Tallahassee, Florida 32399-1600
Web address: www.floridaconservation.org

Snakes may not be collected from, and are fully protected in, Florida's state parks and other state-regulated areas.

Snakes are protected by federal regulations in national wildlife refuges. Check applicable regulations before collecting in national forests. Request federal information from:

Office for Human Relations
United States Fish and Wildlife Service
Department of Interior
Washington, D.C. 20240
Web address: www.fws.org

### Snakes Protected in Florida

The following snake species, subspecies, and populations are protected by Florida law. Note that two types—the eastern indigo snake and the Atlantic salt marsh snake—are also protected by federal law. Permits are needed from each applicable regulatory agency prior to taking, possessing, or otherwise interacting with these species. Two terms, *molesting* and *harassing,* are often used by law enforcement personnel when enforcing laws. The terms are nonspecific and may be broadly interpreted to prevent even photography without a permit, startling a snake into motion, or interrupting its movement.

Key Ring-necked Snake, *Diadophis punctatus acricus,* state protected

Eastern Indigo Snake, *Drymarchon corais couperi,* state and federally protected

Corn Snake, *Elaphe guttata guttata,* Lower Keys populations, state protected

Atlantic Salt Marsh Snake, *Nerodia clarkii taeniata,* state and federally protected

Florida Pine Snake, *Pituophis melanoleucus mugitus,* normal colorations are state protected. Unless otherwise permitted, only a single pine snake per person may be maintained. Amelanistic (albino) morphs are exempted.

Short-tailed Snake, *Stilosoma extenuatum,* state protected

Florida Brown Snake, *Storeria victa,* Keys populations, state protected

Rim Rock Crowned Snake, *Tantilla oolitica,* state protected

Peninsula Ribbon Snake, *Thamnophis sauritus sackenii,* Lower Keys populations, state protected

# Comments on Taxonomy and Classification

The science of classification—of assigning names to and determining affiliations of organisms—is called taxonomy. As in any other discipline, taxonomy includes diverging beliefs, techniques, and applications. Molecular biology has become an important tool in determining the relationships of reptiles and amphibians and has suggested many changes in long-used taxonomic designations. When used in conjunction with other criteria, molecular data usually would seem to provide greater insight to species affinities.

Sadly, there is also a current school of thought holding that allopatrism (noncontiguous populations) equates to speciation. We feel that this may be true in some cases, but that in many instances it is not. This is especially so since many breaks in range are artificial, having been caused by the ministrations of humans since the turn of the twentieth century. We suggest that every species/subspecies must be evaluated on its own merit. Wherever we felt it possible, both the common and scientific names used in this book are those suggested in the publication entitled *Scientific and Standard English Names of Amphibians and Reptiles of North America North of Mexico, with Comments Regarding Confidence in our Understanding* (Crother 2000). This circular is the result of the collaboration of a committee of noted herpetologists and has contributed greatly to nomenclatural stability.

However, we have diverged occasionally. One such case involves the taxonomy of the eastern indigo snake. Despite the fact that it is now allopatric to all other indigo snakes, we have continued to refer to this magnificent serpent as a subspecies. Our opinion on this point may eventually change, but for the moment we have chosen a conservative course.

Recently sweeping taxonomic changes have been suggested for the rat snakes of the eastern United States. Again, while taxonomists argue the pros and cons of the proposed taxonomic redesignation, we will continue for the moment to use the scientific designations by which these snakes have been long known.

Affinities within a family are as controversial as generic and specific nomenclature. We felt the need to follow a single authority when assigning subfamilial affinities, and we chose Harry W. Greene as that authority. There will be time for relevant changes later, when agreement is more general.

In time, taxonomy may again become less conjectural. We can at least hope so.

# Legless Lizards of Florida

The snakes are not the only legless reptiles in Florida. The state is also home to four species of legless lizards of the genus *Ophisaurus* that are often referred to as "glass lizards." The fifth legless lizard is the curious little Florida worm lizard, *Rhineura floridana.* All are found in the same habitats as snakes.

The glass lizards are members of the lizard family Anguidae. All have weakly keeled, shiny scales dorsally and lack enlarged movable scutes (scales) across the belly. In addition, all have movable eyelids and visible ear openings, two characters possessed by no snake. They also have a lateral groove (or fold) along each side of the body. This allows for expansion if a large meal is eaten. When on the surface of the ground (these lizards burrow proficiently) and especially when on a smooth surface such as a paved road, glass lizards move in a rather stiff-appearing side-to-side motion.

All of the glass lizards have a tail that readily breaks (autotomizes) from the body. The original unbroken tail actually comprises between two-thirds to three-quarters of a glass lizard's total length. The tail regrows, but the regenerated member is structurally different and shorter than the original. The tail of the large slender glass lizard is especially fragile. All glass lizards are oviparous. The clutch size averages from 6 to 10 eggs for the smaller species (mimic and island glass lizards) to from 12 to 16 for the two larger species. The female remains with her clutch throughout the incubation period, unusual behavior for a reptile. Hatchling glass lizards are about 6 inches in length.

The eastern glass lizard, *Ophisaurus ventralis,* is the most common and widespread of Florida's species. It is found throughout the state and occurs both in rather dry and in damp habitats. If the tail is original, this big, dark glass lizard can attain a length of 3½ feet, but those seen are often between 18 and 30 inches. Juveniles have 3 well-defined stripes, but adults often lose the vertebral stripe. All striping is above the lateral groove. Old males may lose all traces of striping and take on a gold to turquoise dorsal coloration.

The eastern slender glass lizard, *Ophisaurus attenuatus longicaudus,* is the second most commonly seen species. It occurs throughout the state except in the Everglades. It is a species of sandhills, dry meadows, open pine-oak wood-lands, and well-drained ridges. Although not as stout as the eastern glass lizard when it has an original tail, the slender glass lizard may also attain 3½ feet in length. This species has three prominent stripes and several thinner ones. Some thin stripes occur *below* the lateral groove. Old males develop dark crossbands dorsally. The pattern is strongest anteriorly, where it may partially obliterate the pattern of striping.

Since the island glass lizard, *Ophisaurus compressus,* ranges over almost all of Florida except for the Everglades, it seems curiously misnamed. But the species does occur on islands and keys. It is adult at only 28 inches in length. Of the three stripes, the vertebral stripe is the most prominent. The lateral stripes may be broken into a series of spots anteriorly. No striping is present below the lateral groove. As with other glass lizards, this species darkens and develops dorsal spotting and barring with age. These patterns sometimes obliterate the anterior striping. Lacking fracture planes (specialized areas in the bones of the tail that permit easy breakage), the tail of the island glass lizard is less easily autotomized than those of its kin.

In Florida, the mimic glass lizard, *Ophisaurus mimicus,* is found only in a zigzag band of habitat on the panhandle. It is very similar in appearance to both the slender and the island glass lizards, hence its name. It has fewer than 98 scales along the length of the lateral groove. It has a well-defined vertebral stripe and 3 or 4 stripes along each side above the lateral groove. There may be a poorly defined stripe below the lateral groove.

The little Florida worm lizard is contained in its own suborder and family. It is an amphisbaenid, a group of tropical lizardlike reptiles. It is opalescent whitish-pink to bright pink in color (somewhat paler on the belly) and has a short, blunt, flattened tail that bears numerous hardened tubercular scales. The head scales are hardened and enlarged and are specialized for burrowing. There are no functional eyes. The body scales are arranged in regular rings. The adult size is from 8 to 12 inches in length; 16 inches is the record. Hatchlings are about 4 inches long. This very specialized reptile seldom surfaces but is often turned up by Florida gardeners. It lives in well-drained soils (it is incapable of swimming) along the ridges and in elevated areas across the state from the north side of Lake Okeechobee northward to the Georgia state line.

# NONVENOMOUS Snakes

# Native Snakes

## Colubrine Snakes; Typical or Colubrid Snakes, Family Colubridae

As currently defined, this is a vast and unwieldy assemblage to which most snakes are assigned. The taxonomic assignments are rendered somewhat more workable by the creation of several subfamilies.

Although these snakes are generally described as harmless, the members of several subfamilies have toxic enzymes in their saliva, and some have enlarged teeth at the rear of the upper jaw. All should be handled carefully. Relevant Florida species are the various hog-nosed snakes, some garter snakes, and some water snakes. Although other species—such as the crowned snakes and the ring-necked snakes—are known to bear toxins, these species are too small to be dangerous to humans.

The colubrine snakes vary widely in appearance and lifestyle. Many are short, stocky, and terrestrial. Some are glossy-scaled burrowers. Others are slender speedsters, which may as readily ascend trees as seek refuge on the ground.

## Racers and Related Snakes, Subfamily Colubrinae

This subfamily contains a number of snakes of diverse appearance and habits. In Florida, snakes of five genera are assigned to this group. Among these are some of the fastest snakes found in the United States—the racers and the whip snakes. In addition, there is the big, endangered eastern indigo snake, a racer look-alike that traditionally travels over a range so large that it is almost impossible to offer the species full protection from vehicles and frightened people. The little rough green snake is a fencerow insectivorous species that is so well camouflaged when among greenery that unless it is moving it is almost impossible to see. Finally, there is a group of tiny burrowers that feeds primarily on centipedes and tenebrionid beetle larvae. These are the crowned (or black-headed) snakes. One species, the Florida crowned snake, is itself the sole prey item of the very odd and very rare short-tailed snake. All Florida members of this group are egg-layers.

**Colubrine husbandry** Because most of the larger members of this family are fast, nervous, often feisty, and may not feed well, and the smaller ones are secretive, difficult to feed, and equally difficult to keep—except for the eastern indigo snake (now a regulated species)—the colubrines have never found great favor among snake keepers. Yet, because they are common, species like black racers and rough green snakes are often the species first kept by budding hobbyists.

The snakes in this family are varied in their needs. The racers and the coachwhip snakes should be provided with the largest possible cage and one or more hide boxes. They do not require elevated perches or platforms. The water bowl need be only large enough for drinking. These snakes can be picky eaters, preferring frogs, toads, and lizards over mice. However, most can be induced to eat small mice, especially if scented with a lizard or frog.

The rough green snake is an arboreal insectivore. It should be provided with interlaced branches over which the leafy stems of a vining plant (such as pothos) are draped. Like most arboreal snakes, this species may not recognize a bowl of quiet water as a drinking source. They may drink if the surface of their water supply is roiled with an aquarium air stone but will certainly drink from a drip system or the pendulous droplets when the leaves of the plant in the enclosure are misted. Green snakes dehydrate quickly, but they also quickly develop skin disorders if their enclosure becomes truly wet. Use care. These snakes eat crickets, grasshoppers, spiders, and nontoxic caterpillars. If you collect food for them from the wild, be certain that the bugs come from an insecticide-free area.

The crowned snakes can be kept in small terraria with several inches of smooth-grained sand for burrowing. The bottom layer of sand should be barely moist. These snakes will drink from shallow water dishes. Because they are often difficult to induce to feed and because they desiccate rapidly, crowned snakes are difficult captives. The rim rock crowned snake is a regulated species.

## Racers, Genus *Coluber*

The various subspecies of the black racer are found from the Atlantic to the Pacific coasts but are absent from vast tracts in our southwestern and North Central regions.

Racers are generally thought of as terrestrial serpents, but they climb readily and well.

The majority of the subspecies of the black racer—ten of them—occur in the eastern United States (only two subspecies occur in the American West). Of these, three subspecies may be encountered in Florida. All are noted for their alert demeanor, readiness to bite if molested, and considerable speed. Although most of them are a unicolored black, gray, blue, or brownish-green dorsally when adult, two subspecies have the dark ground color interestingly and variably patterned with spots and blotches of light pigment. The hatchlings and juveniles of most are very strongly patterned with dark dorsal blotches (or crossbars) on a tan to light-brown or grayish ground color.

Hardly could a scientific name be more erroneous than the specific designation *constrictor* that has been bestowed upon this species, for the racers are most emphatically *not* constrictors. They merely grasp their prey and swallow it alive, occasionally making a cursory attempt to immobilize a struggling prey item with a loop of their body. But they never constrict.

All members of this genus are oviparous and produce eggs with a characteristic pebbly shell.

The scales are smooth and arranged in 17 rows at midbody (usually dropping to 15 rows anterior to the vent); the anal plate is divided.

There are three subspecies of racers found in Florida.

Expect to see these snakes in and near open woodlands (especially near clearings or at woodland edges), in pastures and meadows, at bog edges, and in sandlands. They are often seen in suburban and rural yards.

### 1. Brown-chinned Racer
*Coluber constrictor helvigularis*

**Nonvenomous** Like other racers, the brown-chinned racer is feisty but nonvenomous. If cornered, it will strike energetically; if carelessly held, it will bite repeatedly. It can draw blood, but the wounds are insignificant. They should, however, be washed and cleaned with an antiseptic.

**Size** In size, this subspecies is similar to the widespread southern black racer. Most seen are in the range of 3 to 4 feet long, but occasional examples may attain a full 5 feet. Hatchlings are from 8 to 11 inches in length.

**Identification** Like the other races of this far-flung species, the brown-chinned racer has 17 rows of smooth scales and a divided anal plate. Like many other snakes that find their prey visually, the brown-chinned racer has proportionately large eyes. The dorsal ground coloration is black, as is the venter, and the chin and throat are pale brown to variably brown and white. The brown is also present on the lower half of the upper labial scales. The hatchlings have a ground color of gray and bear large, dark-edged, reddish dorsal markings. There are two rows of small reddish markings along each side.

**Behavior** Brown-chinned racers are alert, nervous, visually oriented hunters. They react to nearby movement by freezing, but if approached they will dart quickly away. If cornered they become defensive, rapidly and repeatedly striking. When hunting, these snakes periscope, raising their head well above body level (and often above the tops of the grasses in which they are hunting) to better assess a given situation. The alacrity with which a startled racer disappears into cover can be nearly as disconcerting as its occasional aggressive stance.

**Habitat/Range** This is a snake of shrubby fields, open woodlands, and river- and pond-edge situations. It is often seen crossing the sandy roads that crisscross the Apalachicola National Forest and may be seen in the morning basking along the edges of paved roads.

For all intents and purposes, this racer is restricted in distribution to the immediate vicinity of the Apalachicola National Forest on Florida's central panhandle.

**Abundance** This would seem to be a common snake throughout its small range, but not all have the prominent brown chins for which they are named.

**Prey** Although lizards and frogs seem the principal prey items of the adults, small rodents, nestling birds, and insects are also accepted. Juveniles accept locusts, crickets, cicadas, and non-noxious caterpillars but will also eat suitably sized lizards and frogs.

**Reproduction** A normal clutch seems to consist of from 6 (small females) to 15 or more (large females) rough-shelled eggs. The eggs are concealed in available moisture-retaining debris (beneath decomposing vegetation or manmade litter) and hatch in from 50 to 65 days.

**Similar snakes** See the descriptions of other Florida racers below. The eastern indigo snake has shiny scales. The rough green snake is smaller, bright green dorsally, butter-yellow to white ventrally, and has keeled scales. Hatchling rat snakes have relatively small eyes, a prominently dark-checked belly, and proportionately larger dorsal saddles.

## Other Florida Subspecies

### 2. Everglades Racer
### *Coluber constrictor paludicola*

The Everglades racer differs from the brown-chinned racer primarily in coloration. This snake is restricted in distribution to the Everglades (in its larger past and its present, smaller version), and a population of racers of similar appearance also occurs near Cape Canaveral. Look for it along canals, at pond edge, in shrubby fields, and in sparsely treed woodland. The dorsal ground coloration of the Everglades racer is variable. It is usually a grayish-green to a grayish-brown; it is never jet black. The lower half of the supralabials, the lower labials, the chin, and the venter are bluish-white to bluish-gray. This color sometimes carries over to the lowest row of lateral scales. The hatchlings have a ground color of gray to grayish-tan and are adorned with many dark dorsal saddles. The saddles are very pronounced anteriorly and indistinct to absent posteriorly. The sides are liberally flecked with dark pigment. The venter is lighter. The eyes are proportionately large. This alert snake depends largely on speed to distance itself from potential trouble. It seems less common today than in bygone years.

### 3. Southern Black Racer
### *Coluber constrictor priapus*

The southern black racer undergoes dramatic on-togenetic color changes. Dorsally, laterally, and for most of their venter, the adults are a lustrous, *satiny* (as opposed to shiny) black. The chin is light (usually white with no tan or brown spots), and the white may extend onto the anterior section of the throat. The eye is usually dark but may be yellow or reddish. The hatchlings have a gray-ish ground color, patterned dorsally with a series of reddish to brown blotches. These are best defined anteriorly. Small dark spots occur on the side and on the grayish venter. With growth, the ground color quickly darkens. This ubiquitous snake ranges southward from southern Indiana and south-eastern North Carolina to eastern Louisiana and is found throughout most of Florida, including the Florida Keys.

## Indigo Snakes, Genus *Drymarchon*

This genus is currently in taxonomic disarray. Some researchers believe that what we have long considered a subspecies of a single species is a full species in its own right. At the moment, we decline this speciation by range map and continue to apply trinomial designations to the races of this impressive snake.

The indigo snakes are large, heavy-bodied, and wide-ranging snakes. In today's busy world, the need to wander widely almost invariably brings these snakes into contact with humans and vehicles. All too often the snakes are injured or killed during these encounters. Indigo snakes may bite if provoked, and the strong jaws can produce rather deep lacerations. These should be cleansed and dressed as necessary. Indigos also vibrate their tail noisily, hiss, and flatten their neck vertically in what can be impressive displays.

Indigo snakes are among the largest colubrines and may occasionally ex-ceed a length of 8 feet. They are nonconstrictors, overpowering their prey with their strong jaws and, if necessary, by immobilizing the prey beneath a loop of the body. Prey includes other snakes, lizards, baby turtles, amphib-ians, small mammals, and ground-dwelling birds.

These alert, fast, racerlike serpents utilize all manner of underground lairs, including vacated mammal burrows and the burrows of gopher tortoises. They are active in cold weather but seldom seen in the heat of summer. These are egg-laying snakes.

Look for the indigo snake in scrublands; sandy, open woodlands; coastal dune areas; unmanicured citrus groves; agricultural areas; and along limestone-edged canals.

## 4. Eastern Indigo Snake
### *Drymarchon corais couperi*

**Nonvenomous** Although it looks much like a shiny, heavy-bodied racer, the eastern indigo has a much more mellow disposition. Although if hard-pressed, they may occasionally assume a striking "S" shape, most will allow themselves to be captured and handled without displaying any hostility. However, the indigo snake does have powerful jaws, and a bite from a large specimen will assuredly draw blood. Should this happen, carefully cleanse and dress the wound.

**Size** This is the largest of the southeastern snakes. An average adult is between 5½ and 6½ feet in length, and the record size is 8 feet 7½ inches! Hatchlings may vary from 1½ to 2 feet in length.

**Identification** Although the belly color may vary, the dorsal color of the adult eastern indigo is an overall shiny black with indigo overtones. The snout and cheeks may be mostly black or strongly orange-red. The belly of the adult indigo may be mostly black (with a red-orange to whitish chin) to as much as 50 percent red (anteriorly). Although age-related color and pattern changes are not as overt as those that occur on the racers, they are still noticeable on the indigo snake. Hatchlings may have an almost completely orange head, be quite blue in ground color, and have prominent light banding. With growth, these colors fade; by the time the indigo is 2½ feet in length, it has assumed its adult coloration.

The shiny scales are smooth on females, but adult males have some of the dorsal scales weakly keeled. Scales are in 17 rows, and the anal plate is undivided.

**Behavior** The eastern indigo snake is an active and territorial snake that utilizes an immense range. Males—especially during the breeding season—defend their territory from encroachment by rivals. Thanks to advanced tracking methods, much about the home range and territoriality of the indigo snake has been learned, relearned, and confirmed. Other aspects of its home life remain enigmatic. The range of the adult indigo snake varies with the weather. During warm weather, adult males are known to utilize ranges that cover an average of 370 acres! Many territories are much larger. During cold weather, the snakes are comparative homebodies, occupying ranges of 50 or fewer acres. Indigo snakes occupy the burrows of armadillos and gopher tortoises, stump holes, or almost any other safe haven when resting. They seem to know their home ranges intricately, if possible heading straight to safe haven when threatened. Indigos respond in an alert manner to most visual stimuli, from the small movements of a frog or rat to the approach of a human.

Although most indigo snakes will attempt to escape if approached by a predator (including a human), some—if truly surprised—will stand their ground. With head, neck, and anterior body held in an "S" shape well above the ground, a frightened indigo may strike repeatedly and vibrate its tail. If the opportunity presents itself, the snake will turn and disappear quickly into surrounding cover.

**Habitat/Range** This is a wide-ranging and adaptable snake. It may be encountered in habitats such as fields, meadows, pastures, open woodlands, and large agricultural areas. It is also found in old citrus groves or along canals, habitats that often harbor populations of the amphibians, reptiles, and small mammals upon which this huge snake feeds. This is a terrestrially oriented snake. When preparing to shed, it shelters beneath natural and manmade debris or in burrows or other such lairs.

This threatened snake ranges throughout Florida and is found rarely in adjacent Alabama and eastern Georgia.

**Abundance** Once a relatively common species, the eastern indigo snake is now seldom seen (although it does remain rather common in suitable pockets of habitat) and is considered a federally threatened species.

**Prey** Frogs, lizards, smaller snakes, rodents, birds—all are grist for the mill of this magnificent snake. When hunting, an eastern indigo snake often periscopes, elevating its head above grass levels and searching visually for its prey.

**Reproduction** Although the males of many snakes are moderately agonistic at breeding time, male indigo snakes are excessively so. Reproductively conditioned males fight savagely and may inflict severe wounds. From 3 to 12 eggs are laid. Like a racer's eggs (but ever so much larger), those of the indigo have pebbly shells.

**Similar snakes** Black-phase eastern hog-nosed snakes have a sharpened and vaguely upturned rostral scale and dull scales. Black racers have a white chin and a satiny (not a shiny) finish on their scales.

## Whipsnakes, Genus *Masticophis*

These snakes are closely allied to the snakes of the racer genus, *Coluber*. The whipsnakes are alert, slender serpents that often seek prey by periscoping their head above the surrounding grasses and ground plants. Their vision is apparently acute, and the whipsnakes seem to rely as much on visual as on chemical cues when pursuing prey. All manner of prey—from frogs, lizards, and smaller snakes (including those of their own kind)to small mammals and birds—are opportunistically eaten. Because of their response to visual cues, whipsnakes (coachwhips, in the Southeast) readily locate and predate the nests of birds in shrubs and low trees. The food is not constricted.

Many of the whipsnakes (which are well speciated in the American West) are of somewhat similar appearance. The scale row count varies from 15 to 17. The scales are smooth; the anal plate is divided. Identification in Florida is easier—there is only a single species.

While rather narrow (bluntly lance-shaped), the head is deep and well defined from the slim neck.

Although they would prefer a rapid and uneventful escape to a standoff, if cornered, whipsnakes vibrate their tail, assume a striking "S" shape, and will bite strongly. Some may even approach an offending object (such as a human) as they strike. Whipsnakes are nonvenomous. Bite wounds should be cleansed and treated if necessary.

All of the whipsnakes (and racers) lay eggs with a characteristic granular shell.

Look for these sandland and scrubland speedsters in the proximity of rangeland, old citrus groves, scrub-oak ridges, and other similar areas.

## 5. Eastern Coachwhip Snake
### *Masticophis flagellum flagellum*

**Nonvenomous** This is a feisty snake that will bite readily if cornered or molested and will sometimes even approach an antagonist. A bite can draw blood, but the snake is entirely devoid of venom. Clean the wound and apply a dressing.

**Size** Because of its excessive slenderness, the eastern coachwhip is often judged to be smaller than its actual length. Although it may occasionally attain a length of 8½ feet, a more usual length is between 5 and 6½ feet long. The very slender hatchlings are usually between 13 and 16 inches in length.

**Identification** Ontogenetic changes in this racer relative are noticeable but not as marked as in the racers themselves. Hatchling coachwhips have a strongly light-and-dark patterned face and dark dorsal crossbands. These fade with age and growth. There are several adult color phases, but on all coachwhips, the head is the darkest and the tail the lightest. One phase is a solid sandy tan (sometimes the top of the head is dark). A second is black anteriorly, fading to tan about a third of the way back. This phase often has the light scales outlined with dark, a characteristic that produces the braided look of an old coach whip and has given the snake its common name. A third phase with a solid black body and a (usually) dull reddish tail is also known.

These snakes have a belly that may be tan, grayish tan, or very dark. Again, the color below the tail is usually the lightest. Some striping may be visible on the throat. The eyes are large, and widened supraocular scales shade the eyes and give the snake a sullen look. The eye is usually yellow or reddish. The scales are smooth; in 17 rows (13 rows just anterior to the vent—an important factor when trying to decide whether you have a black coachwhip or a black racer in hand); and the anal plate is divided.

**Behavior** The eastern coachwhip is one of Florida's most active and speediest snakes. It responds in an alert manner to most visual stimuli, from the small movement of a frog or mouse to the approach of a human.

Although most coachwhips will attempt to escape if approached by human or large predator, some will stand their ground or even make their way toward a threatening object. They do so with head, neck, and anterior body in an "S" shape held well above the ground, often feinting and striking, and vibrating their tail in dried vegetation as they approach. This can be a daunting experience to someone unfamiliar with the ways of snakes.

**Habitat/Range** In Florida—where it ranges over the entire mainland from the southernmost tip of the Florida peninsula to Escambia and Nassua Counties in the west and northeast—this is a snake of sandhills and scrublands. Although wide-ranging and adaptable, the coachwhip is no longer seen with the regularity it once was. However, it still may be encountered in such habitats as suburban fencerows, old fields, sandy pastures, open woodlands, sprawling prairies, and old citrus groves. It may even be found in sandy areas within sight of the ocean. The coachwhip is usually seen on the ground but readily ascends shrubs and shrubby trees, at times climbing high above the ground. It shelters beneath natural and manmade debris or in burrows when preparing to shed.

North and west of Florida, it may be found from central North Carolina to southeastern Kansas and eastern Texas.

**Abundance** Once a commonly encountered snake, the eastern coachwhip is now less regularly seen in Florida. However, it is far from being an uncommon species.

**Prey** Frogs, lizards, and smaller snakes are the preferred prey of this snake. Some specimens will also eat baby rodents, nestling birds, and even insects. When actively hunting, eastern coachwhips often search for their prey by periscoping—lifting their head above the level of the grass and searching visually for movement.

**Reproduction** From 5 to 12 eggs comprise a normal clutch. The eggs are secluded beneath or in moisture-retaining logs or debris of either natural or manmade origin; they also may be laid in an unused mammal or reptile burrow. The incubation duration varies from about 48 to 65 days, depending on warmth and moisture. An adult female was coiled around one clutch of 10 eggs found beneath a fallen signboard in Central Florida.

**Similar snakes** The racers of Florida could be confused with a black-phase coachwhip, but the racers are smaller and have 15 scale rows just anterior to the vent. Baby racers have large dorsal saddles. The dorsal markings of the coachwhip are narrower. Baby rat snakes have small eyes, a checkered belly, and large dorsal blotches.

## Green Snakes, Genus *Opheodrys*

The green snakes are characteristically the brightest green of any American serpent. The venter of both is white to yellowish or of the palest whitish-green. Only a single species, the rough green snake, occurs in Florida.

The rough green snake is a slender arborealist that feeds on caterpillars, crickets, and spiders. Although often associated with tall grasses, shrubs, and low trees, rough green snakes have been found high in the canopy.

This little racer-relative has acute vision. It is an oviparous species.

The scales are keeled and in 17 rows; the anal plate is divided.

If startled, a rough green snake will indulge in a mouth-gaping defensive display but is reluctant to bite.

This snake may be found in all habitats except dense woodland. They are most often found in vines and shrubs along the edges of highways, meadows, and pastures; in fencerow vines; in gardens when insecticides are not used; and in other such overgrown areas. Tangles of brambles and shrubs along canal banks and lake edges are also favored.

## 6. Rough Green Snake
### *Opheodrys aestivus*

**Nonvenomous** This easygoing little snake is entirely devoid of venom and usually cannot be induced to bite.

**Size** This is a very slender snake that is typically between 2 and 3 feet in length. Occasional specimens attain a length of 3¾ feet. The hatchlings usually measure about 7½ inches in length.

**Identification** Ontogenetic changes in this racer-relative are obvious but occur so rapidly that they are seldom noticed. Hatchlings are bluish-green to dull-green, but by the time the postnatal skin shedding has occurred (only a few days after hatching), these snakes have already assumed their leaf-green coloration. Interestingly, dead specimens quickly lose their green coloration and take on an overall grayish coloration.

There may be no other snake in Florida as readily identifiable as an adult rough green snake. This is the only snake in the state that is a vivid leaf-green above and pale-yellow to white below. The upper lip is also edged with white or yellow. The yellow eye is large. The scales are keeled, in 17 rows, and the anal plate is divided.

**Behavior** The rough green snake is usually slow and methodical in its movements. If approached, it becomes quiescent and depends on its color to camouflage it in the vegetation. Look for it among vines and low shrubs (we have a fair population in our suburban Gainesville, Florida, backyard), but unless the snake is moving it is likely to be overlooked.

**Habitat/Range** From Key West northward, the rough green snake occurs throughout Florida. It also ranges over much of the eastern United States, from central New Jersey to eastern Kansas and eastern Texas. Although it is wide-ranging and adaptable, insecticides seem to have taken a toll on the insectivorous rough green snake. It is no longer seen with the regularity it once was. However, it still may be encountered in such habitats as suburban fencerows and gardens, old fields, woodland edges, and along vine-covered railroad beds. The rough green snake is usually seen in shrubs and among vines. When preparing to shed its skin, this snake may take shelter beneath natural or manmade debris.

**Abundance** Although still a common species, the rough green snake is now less regularly seen in Florida than it once was.

**Prey** This is an insectivorous snake. Caterpillars, spiders, crickets, and grasshoppers comprise the prey items most commonly eaten by this snake. Like racers, these alert snakes often periscope while searching for their prey.

**Reproduction** From 5 to 12 eggs make up a normal clutch. The eggs are secluded beneath or in moisture-retaining vegetation—alive or dead. The eggs' shells are rough—not pebbly (like those of the related racers).

**Similar snakes** None in Florida.

## Crowned Snakes, Genus *Tantilla*

In the Southeast, the snakes of this genus are diminutive burrowers. Farther to the west, they are larger but equally secretive. Most are characterized by a black crown and sometimes a black nape. The head and neck color may or may not be separated by a light band.

The unicolored dorsum is often the color of the substrate on which these snakes are found. There is no loreal scale, an important identification fact.

The eyes are proportionately small, and the head and neck are the same diameter as the body.

These are snakes of sandy, well-drained areas and may occasionally be found beneath flat stones and building debris. They vary by species from common and fairly well known—despite their persistent secrecy—to rare and poorly understood.

The scales of these oviparous snakes are in 15 rows; the anal plate is divided.

Traditionally, the most reliable identifying characteristics have been considered to be the shape of the posterior edge of the dark crown and whether or not the crowned snake in question has a light collar. While these must be considered, there is actually much variation in crown characteristics even within a subspecies. Rely also on range to identify these snakes.

The reproductive biology of the snakes in the genus *Tantilla* is unusual, even if of no consequence to a field observer. These snakes have two functional ovaries but only a single functional oviduct. Eggs formed in the left ovary are shunted into the functional right oviduct for deposition. Because spermatogenesis occurs at a different time of year from ovulation, sperm storage is necessary. Following mating, sperm is in the nonfunctional, vestigial section of the left oviduct until fertilization of the ripe ovum occurs.

Although possessing a toxic saliva, the crowned snakes are reluctant to bite and are considered harmless to man.

These snakes may be expected in regions of sandy soil. Open woodlands, scrubby ridges, and backyards all provide suitable habitats.

### 7. Southeastern Crowned Snake
*Tantilla coronata*

**Very mildly venomous** Although the saliva of this snake is mildly toxic, the snake is entirely harmless to humans and usually cannot be induced to bite.

**Size** This tiny snake is often hardly larger than a big earthworm. From 7 to 12½ inches is the adult size. Hatchlings are about 3 inches in length.

**Identification** The rear of the black crown is gently curved, but there may be short rearward exten-

sions following the sutures of the parietal shields. The black of the head may reach the mouth-line, or a light supralabial streak may be present. A light collar followed by a large black nape-blotch is present. The dorsal color is tan to reddish-tan, usually closely mimicking the color of the soil in which this snake dwells. The belly is an opalescent white to pale yellow or pink. This slender snake has 15 rows of smooth scales and a divided anal plate.

**Behavior** This diminutive snake is nervous, moves quickly when uncovered, and may thrash from side to side in its evasive attempts. It is an accomplished burrower and is seldom encountered above ground.

**Habitat/Range** In Florida, this snake is distributed over most of the panhandle. Outside of Florida, the southeastern crowned snake occurs as far north as western Kentucky and central Virginia and as far west as eastern Louisiana. Habitats are many and varied. Soil moisture can vary from moderate (not wet, though) to very dry, and the ground cover may be woodlands, scrubland, or grassland—the latter including urban fields and yards.

**Abundance** Because of its persistent burrowing habits, actual population statistics are difficult to obtain. However, this is probably not an uncommon snake.

**Prey** Centipedes seem to be the primary prey item, and the toxins of this little snake soon overcome and immobilize these multisegmented, biting chilopods. Insects and their larvae are also eaten.

**Reproduction** Eggs may number from 1 to 5 in each clutch. See comments regarding reproduction in the discussion of the genus *Tantilla*, page 43.

**Similar snakes** Use range to identify this species. This is the only crowned snake in the Florida panhandle.

## 8. Rim Rock Crowned Snake
*Tantilla oolitica*

**Very mildly venomous** The saliva of the rim rock crowned snake is mildly toxic, but the snake is entirely harmless to humans and usually cannot be induced to bite.

**Size** This tiny snake is often hardly larger than a big earthworm. From 7 to 9 inches in length is the adult size.

**Identification** The black of the head extends well

beyond the head scales onto the nape. There is no light collar. The body color varies from pale whitish-tan to a rather rich tannish-brown.

**Behavior** This diminutive snake is nervous, moves quickly when uncovered, and may thrash from side to side in its evasive attempts. It is an accomplished burrower and is seldom encountered. Nothing is known with certainty about its lifestyle.

**Habitat/Range** While most of Dade County's former upland habitat is now under parking lots and shopping centers (not to mention private dwellings), this little snake continues to turn up on occasion. The most recently found examples have come from some of the more southerly of the Upper Keys. Researcher John Decker has found rim rock crowned snakes in piles of damp discarded clothing as well as beneath rocks. This is the only crowned snake known from southeastern Florida and the Keys. It ranges southward from Dade County and is sparsely distributed throughout the Upper Keys.

**Abundance** Unknown, but thought to be rare. This is a protected species in Florida.

**Prey** Captives have eaten small centipedes but have refused spiders and insect larvae. Its food in the wild is unknown.

**Reproduction** Other than the fact that this is an oviparous snake, nothing is known with certainty about the reproductive biology of this species.

**Similar snakes** Use range to identify the rim rock crowned snake. It is the only species of this genus to occur from Dade County southward.

## 9. Central Florida Crowned Snake
*Tantilla relicta neilli*

**Very mildly venomous** As with the other Florida *Tantilla,* the saliva of this snake is mildly toxic. Despite this, the snake is entirely harmless to humans and usually cannot be induced to bite.

**Size** This tiny snake is often hardly larger than a big earthworm. From 7 to 9 inches is the adult size. Hatchlings are about 2.75 inches in length.

**Identification** The black of the head extends well beyond the head scales onto the nape. There is usually no light collar, but where the collar would be, if present, may be indicated by an upward notch in the black pigment at the lower sides of the rear of the head. The body color is sandy tan to reddish-brown, usually closely simulating the color of the soils on which the snake is living. There are 15 rows of smooth scales and a divided anal plate.

**Behavior** This diminutive snake is nervous and attempts to quickly recover itself when uncovered. If grasped, the snake wriggles strongly in its attempts to escape. It is often found beneath human-generated surface debris such as construction rubble and old boards and like its relatives is often raked from just beneath the surface of the soil when the weather is warm and damp. At times of drought it burrows deeply, following the moisture line, and is seldom seen.

**Habitat/Range** The range of this fossorial snake arcs inland and upward from the vicinity of Tampa on the west coat to the vicinity of Lakeland, then north to Jennings (Hillsborough County to Polk County to Madison County). Found virtually to the Georgia state line, the range of *T. r. neilli* does not seem to extend into that state. This is a widely distributed crowned snake that utilizes many microhabitats. It is often raked from just beneath the surface of the soil when the weather is warm and damp, but it probably burrows deeply to avoid excessive heat, cold, or drought.

**Abundance** Because of its persistent burrowing habits, actual population statistics are difficult to obtain. However, this is probably a common snake.

**Prey** Centipedes seem to be the primary prey item, and the toxins of this little snake soon overcome and immobilize these multisegmented, biting chilopods. Insects and their larvae are probably also eaten.

**Reproduction** Eggs may number from 1 to 5 in each clutch. See comments regarding reproduction in the discussion of the genus *Tantilla*, page 43.

**Similar snakes** See descriptions of other races of this species below. Use range as an identification tool. Where this form abuts the range of the peninsula crowned snake, specimens of intermediate appearance are often seen. The peninsula crowned snake usually has a light collar, separating the black of the head from that of the nape.

ADDITIONAL FLORIDA SPECIES

### 10. Coastal Dunes Crowned Snake
*Tantilla relicta pamlica*

The rear of the crown of the coastal dunes crowned snake is gently curved, but it may have short rearward extensions following the sutures of the parietal shields. The medial projection may be especially prominent vertebrally, where it may narrowly break the light collar, connecting the black of the head to the black nape-patch. The body color is sandy tan to reddish-brown, usually closely simulating the color of the soils on which the snake is living. This race ranges along Florida's east coast from Palm Beach County north to northern Brevard, and perhaps southern Volusia, Counties. It is the only crowned snake found along Florida's central east coast.

### 11. Peninsula Crowned Snake
*Tantilla relicta relicta*

This snake usually has the black of the head separated from the black of the nape by a light collar. The body color is sandy tan to reddish-brown, usually closely simulating the color of the soils on which the snake is living. This race ranges to the east and south of the Central Florida crowned snake. The peninsula crowned snake occurs in three disjunct ranges. The main range extends southward from near Melrose in the north to Lake Placid in the south, with a midway extension westward to Tampa (southern Clay County to Highlands County to Hillsborough County). It also occurs near the coast in Sarasota, Charlotte, and Lee (and probably Collier) Counties.

# Dipsadine Snakes

## Pine Woods Snake, Subfamily Dipsadinae

The snakes of this family are grouped here because of hemipenial morphology. If grasped by the tail, some members of the family autotomize these members readily. Unlike the tails of many lizards, the tail of these snakes does not regenerate. All members of this subfamily have enlarged teeth at the rear of the upper jaw and have weak venom to help them overpower their prey. This subfamily is of primarily neotropical distribution. In fact, only one species of one genus occurs in the United States. This single small snake, *Rhadinea flavilata,* has a curiously disjunct series of ranges from northeastern North Carolina to eastern Louisiana.

## Pine Woods Snake, Genus *Rhadinea*

The pine woods snake is a species of the southeastern and Gulf coastal plains. It is small, secretive, and oviparous. While typically a species of the pine flatwoods—where it hides beneath or in decomposing fallen trunks, mats of vegetation, and roadside debris—it also turns up rather regularly in damp backyards and old fields, especially beneath urban litter. In old texts, this species was referred to as the "yellow-lipped snake."

The smooth scales are arranged in 17 rows; the anal plate is divided. The dorsum is earthen brown to russet (darkest vertebrally), and the belly is a pale yellowish-white.

The mildly toxic saliva helps in overcoming the small lizards and frogs on which this snake species feeds. It is considered harmless to man.

The pine woods snake is found beneath debris in woodlands or, more infrequently, at the wooded edges of pastures and yards.

**Dipsadine husbandry** This secretive snake can be kept in small terraria with several inches of smooth-grained sand for burrowing, atop which is a layer of dried leaves. The bottom layer of sand should be barely moist. These snakes will drink from shallow water dishes. The pine woods snake is often a difficult captive but may eat tiny frogs or lizards.

## 12. Pine Woods Snake
*Rhadinea flavilata*

**Very mildly venomous** In this volume, we have described many snakes as secretive. Although the term fits many snakes rather well, it is more suitable for some than others. The little pine woods snake is truly secretive. In fact, the neotropical species of this genus are referred to as leaf-litter snakes, because the niche for which they have evolved is under and amidst the leaf litter of the rainforests. This snake produces a toxin that effectively quiets its prey. It is entirely harmless to humans and can seldom be induced to bite.

**Size** This tiny snake is often only the length and diameter of a pencil. Eight to 12 inches is the normal adult length of the pine woods snake, and the record size is a hair less than 16 inches. Hatchlings are about 5 inches long.

**Identification** The dorsal color is yellowish-brown to reddish-brown, darkest vertebrally. The chin is white. The venter is off-white, pale yellow, or pale-green, and unmarked. There is a dark eye-stripe, and the upper labials are light in color (but are seldom even vaguely yellowish) and bear a variable amount of dark flecking. The smooth scales are in 17 rows, and the anal plate is divided.

**Behavior** We have never found this snake surface-active. All seen have been beneath debris both by day and night. In most cases, the snakes were not particularly nervous when their lair was invaded, allowing themselves to be lifted and handled without showing defensive belligerence. However, one example from near Tampa flattened its head and struck repeatedly (apparently with closed mouth, for I never was bitten) as my hand neared it.

**Habitat/Range** In Florida, this species has a primary and a disjunct secondary range. It is found from the latitude of Lake Okeechobee on the southern peninsula northward throughout the rest of the peninsula. A tiny, apparently disjunct population occurs in Walton and Okaloosa Counties. Unlike many of Florida's small snakes that prefer dry habitats, the pine woods snake is more at home in woodlands that are well on the damp side. In shaded damp and humid woodlands, look for this snake beneath any manner of surface debris—both natural and human-generated.

**Abundance** Is this snake merely secretive and overlooked, or is it not often seen because it is truly uncommon? Despite traipsing through the woodlands of Florida for more than four decades, we still are not able to accurately answer that question. We have found one pine woods snake here, another there, and a third elsewhere. The findings were scattered over a period of years. Then we would return to a site at another time and find three or four of the little snakes in short order. Our yard in Gainesville, Florida, is a perfect example. As we are wont to do wherever we live, we "seeded" the yard with pieces of tin or boards. For the first several years, we could expect to find a southern ring-necked snake or a Florida red-bellied snake when we checked beneath the cover. Then, in the summer of our fifth year, we began finding pine woods snakes beneath the cover, and by the end of the season we had found six. We had never had an inkling that the snakes occurred there. In year six, we had great expectations of finding more pine woods snakes. We were wrong. Again ring-necked snakes and red-bellied snakes were found, but we never saw the first pine woods snake, nor have we seen one since. Secretive or rare? In our area at least, we would definitely opt for the former.

**Prey** Small amphibians and lizards are eaten.

**Reproduction** A clutch of 3 eggs, found beneath a board in June, hatched after being observed for 51 days. How long the eggs had been there before being found is unknown.

**Similar snakes** Earth snakes, brown snakes, and red-bellied snakes have keeled scales. Crowned snakes have gray to black heads.

## Lampropeltine Snakes

### Kingsnakes, Rat Snakes, Bullsnakes, and Relatives, Subfamily Lampropeltinae

In Florida, there are five genera of lampropeltine snakes. Besides the well-known rat snakes, pine snakes, and kingsnakes, there are the scarlet snakes and the short-tailed snakes. Of these, the rat snakes, pine snakes, and kingsnakes are powerful constrictors that kill their prey before eating it. The short-tailed snake is a weak constrictor, a prey specialist that merely tries to keep the small snakes on which it feeds from coiling into unmanageable positions after being grasped. The reptile-egg-eating scarlet snakes have no need to constrict and seldom even coil tightly.

The lampropeltine snakes are the favorites of herpetoculturists, and tens of thousands of these snakes are bred in captivity every year. Aberrant, or designer, colors and patterns have been developed in many species. Despite their very different appearance, the kingsnakes, pine snakes, and rat snakes have been hybridized by hobbyist-breeders, and in most cases the offspring produced have proven reproductively viable. This viability challenges one principal definition of the current species concept, which states that the young of two species cannot reproduce.

Snakes of this subfamily occur not only in Florida but also widely over North America and Asia. A few types are present in the neotropics.

**Lampropeltine husbandry** The lizard-egg-eating scarlet snakes are very difficult to keep. They should not be collected. The short-tailed snake is a regulated species that must not be collected. The Florida pine snake is regulated, but with a quota. Check the current regulations of the Florida Fish and Wildlife Conservation Commission. The rat snakes, kingsnakes, and pine snakes are pretty, hardy, and easily kept.

The snakes in this family all have very similar captive needs. All should be provided with the largest possible cage and one or more hide boxes. Cage tops (or doors) *must* be tight and lockable. These snakes do not *require* elevated perches or platforms, but the rat snakes (including the corn snake) will often use them if they are available. The water bowl need be only large enough for drinking, but if a larger one is provided, many of these snakes will soak, especially when preparing to shed their skin. These snakes are usually not picky eaters. The hatchlings of some species may prefer frogs or lizards for the first few meals but will usually accept baby mice. Large lampropeltine snakes will eat rodents (and/or baby chicks).

## Scarlet Snake, Genus *Cemophora*

This genus, containing only one species, is a beautiful burrower of the southeastern coastal plain. Even when severely provoked, it is almost impossible to induce the scarlet snake to bite. It is entirely nonvenomous. The scarlet snake may surface in the evening or after dark on warm nights, or when driven from its burrows by heavy rains. The scarlet snake is clad in bands (*not* rings, which encircle the body) of red, black, and white or yellow. The two traffic-light caution colors—yellow and red—are separated by bands of black. The head is narrow and not overly distinct from the neck; the pointed snout is red. The belly is an unbanded off-white to yellow. The smooth scales are arranged in 19 rows, and the anal plate is undivided. Two subspecies of this egg-laying snake occur in Florida.

Despite its affinities to the king snakes, pine snakes, and rat snakes—powerful constrictors all—the scarlet snake, which feeds primarily on reptile eggs, is not a noted constrictor.

This snake may be found by day beneath surface debris but is more often seen after dark when it becomes surface-active. They often cross trails and roadways in sandy areas of scrub or open woodlands.

### 13. Florida Scarlet Snake
*Cemophora coccinea coccinea*

**Nonvenomous** Not only is this snake nonvenomous, but it is almost impossible to induce it to bite.
**Size** Normally between 14 and 20 inches in length when adult, occasional examples may attain a length of 30 inches.
**Identification** This is a brilliantly banded snake with a pure white belly. The pointed snout is

bright red, which is also usually the predominant body color as well. The yellow (or white) and black bands are narrower than the red. The black and yellow bands may actually be true bands or may be little more than saddles. The color sequence is red-black-yellow-black-red. Although seemingly gaudy, the aposematic pattern is disruptive when the snake is moving quickly. This subspecies normally has 7 supralabial scales, 19 rows of smooth scales, and an undivided anal plate.

**Behavior** The scarlet snake is a gentle snake that can seldom be induced to bite. It is generally not seen above ground until well after dark. It occasionally may be found by day by turning ground-surface debris, and it may also be induced to diurnal activity by the lowering barometric pressure accompanying heavy rains.

**Habitat/Range** The Florida scarlet snake inhabits areas of loose soils on the southern two-thirds of the Florida peninsula. Look for it in sandy scrub as well as in elevated hammocks, in pinelands, and on dry prairies.

**Abundance** This is another of the many snakes of Florida that, although quite common, are so secretive that they are seldom seen. This snake may be seen after dark—sometimes in numbers—crawling on the sandy woodland floor or crossing sand-country roadways.

**Prey** Contrary to anecdotal accounts of the scarlet snake accepting lizards, smaller snakes, and even newborn mice as prey, none of the many specimens we have observed has voluntarily done so. Rather, all held out until the eggs of lizards or small snakes were offered. These they voluntarily ate after tongue-flicking them extensively. Feeding these snakes is essentially impossible.

**Reproduction** Like all other North American members of this subfamily, the Florida scarlet snake is oviparous. Clutches are small, usually numbering fewer than 8 eggs. The hatchlings are just under 6 inches in length.

**Similar snakes** Although the scarlet kingsnake and the coral snake also seem patterned in red, black, and yellow bands, on these two snakes the colors are actually rings that completely encircle the body—belly included. Also, the coral snake has the two traffic-light caution colors, red and yellow, touching—not separated by black. The northern scarlet snake usually has only 6 upper labial scales.

ADDITIONAL FLORIDA SUBSPECIES

## 14. Northern Scarlet Snake
### *Cemophora coccinea copei*

This snake is much like its southern relative in appearance. The northern scarlet snake is brilliantly banded in red, yellow (or white), and black. The belly is pure white. The pointed snout is red. Either the red or the yellow may be the predominant dorsal color, but it is usually the red. Often the bands of all colors are of nearly the same width. The color sequence is red-black-yellow-black-red. Although seemingly gaudy, the aposematic pattern is disruptive, and the snake blends quite well with its background. This subspecies normally has 6 supralabial scales, 19 rows of smooth scales, and an undivided anal plate. This race inhabits areas of loose soils on the northern one-third of the Florida peninsula and throughout the panhandle. Look for it in sandy scrub as well as in elevated hammocks, in pinelands, and on dry prairies.

## Rat Snakes, Genus *Pantherophis* (*Elaphe*)

The genus *Pantherophis* (*Elaphe*) is represented in Florida by two species—the corn snake and several races of the black rat snake.

These are among the most popular snakes with herpetoculturists. Tens of thousands are now bred annually by American reptile enthusiasts.

As a group, adult American rat snakes have weakly keeled dorsal and dorsolateral scales and unkeeled lateral scales. The juveniles of all lack scale keels. The number of scale rows varies both by species and individually. The corn snakes have the scales arranged in 27 or 29 rows, and the black rat snake and its relatives have from 25 to 33 rows. The anal plate is divided. All American species in this genus are oviparous.

If looked at in cross section, these snakes would be seen to be rounded on top, to have weakly convex sides, and to have a flattened venter. Rat snakes are agile climbers that can ascend virtually straight up a tree with only moderately rough bark and can ascend even smooth-barked trees (though with more difficulty).

Because of their propensity for farm and barnyards—especially near piles of debris or unused buildings—farmers often refer to the various rat snakes as chicken snakes. While there is no denying that a visiting rat snake will eat an occasional baby chick (and even more rarely, an egg or two), it is usually the ready availability of rodents—the preferred prey of these powerful constrictors—that draws them to farmyards or urban settings.

Many rat snakes undergo marked ontogenetic changes. At hatching, the juveniles of all are strongly blotched or cross-barred. With age and growth, many lose their juvenile pattern, becoming instead strongly striped.

Juvenile rat snakes usually feed on small lizards and tree frogs, while the adults of most consume rodents, rabbits, and some birds.

Most rat snakes kill or immobilize their prey animals by constriction. Some, however, will fail to constrict small items. This is especially true of the fox snakes, both of which often pursue rodents into their burrows where constriction would be impossible. We have noted that instead of constricting, captive fox snakes often immobilize their prey by pressing it against the side of their cage with a body curve. Such a technique would probably work very well in the narrow confines of a rodent burrow.

If carelessly handled, most wild rat snakes will bite. Some strike savagely and repeatedly. Many quickly become accustomed to handling and become very tractable.

Based primarily on molecular data, Frank Burbrink has recently (2001) suggested an overhaul of the long-standing taxonomy for the *Pantherophis* (*Elaphe*) *obsoleta* group. He has proposed four clades, naming them *Pantherophis* (*Elaphe*) *alleghaniensis* (the eastern rat snake) in the east; *P.* (*E.*) *spiloides* (the central rat snake) next west; *P.* (*E.*) *obsoleta* (the western rat snake) from west of the Mississippi; and *P.* (*E.*) *bairdi* (Baird's rat snake) from central Texas and northern Mexico. As defined, the yellow and the Everglades rat snakes would become *P.* (*E.*) *alleghaniensis,* while the gray rat snake would be divided between *P.* (*E.*) *alleghaniensis* (northwestern peninsula and eastern panhandle) and *P.* (*E.*) *spiloides* (western panhandle).

Until we see how these conclusions are accepted by herpetologists, we will retain the old taxonomy here.

Rat snakes are habitat generalists. They may be found in woodlands, rural and suburban yards, unkempt groves, overgrown areas near warehouses, along canals, and in many other habitats.

## 15. Corn Snake
### *Pantherophis (Elaphe) guttata guttata*

**Nonvenomous** This is probably the most thoroughly understood snake of Florida, if not the world. It is a beautiful constrictor that is usually of good disposition, but that may strike and bite, especially when preparing to shed its skin. A large corn snake can produce lacerations that may bleed freely. If bitten, the wound should be cleansed and dressed as a wound from any source would be.

**Size** This snake is of variable size. In the Miami area—where its diet often consists largely of lizards—the corn snake may be mature at 26 to 30 inches. Elsewhere, where its diet is more varied, a length of more than 4 feet is often attained. The largest corn snakes can exceed 6 feet in length. Hatchlings are about 8½ inches in length.

**Identification** Although corn snakes are usually readily recognizable throughout their range, they do vary widely in dorsal color.

The corn snakes of the east coast are usually tan or red with black-edged, deeper red blotches. The species seems particularly brightly colored from eastern North Carolina southward to northeastern Florida. Specimens from the more westerly portion of the range often have an olive wash over both ground color and blotches. Contrast between blotches and ground color is lessened.

Corn snakes are particularly variable in Florida. A large segment of a population in northeastern Florida has much-reduced black and a rosy wash over the entire dorsum. A few very red (erythristic) corn snakes lacking virtually all of the black (both dorsally and ventrally) have been found in this population.

Interior southwestern Florida is home to a significant population of corn snakes that lack virtually all red pigment. Areas of yellow are often visible on the sides of the neck. Except for the yellow highlights, these anerythristic (melanistic) corn snakes have a grayish ground color with dark-edged brown dorsal saddles. The dorsal saddles are often outlined in black, and the belly is normally black-and-white checkered.

The corn snakes of central western Florida often have a reduced amount of black pigment both dorsally and ventrally, and those of South Florida are typified by a silvery gray dorsum with black-edged, deep-red saddles.

The corn snakes of the Florida Keys (discussed below) are equally variable. Despite having once been referred to as "rosy rat snakes," many are anything but rosy. While the saddles of all vary from rosy to dark red, the ground color may be olive, light rose-red, silver, or, more rarely, brownish. There is a tendency for all black pigment to be reduced, and the spearpoint atop the head is often indistinct.

The weakly keeled scales of all corn snakes are in 27 (normal) or 29 rows, and the anal plate is divided.

**Behavior** Although they can climb well, corn snakes tend to be more terrestrially inclined than Florida's other rat snakes. They may bask low in the limbs of an Australian pine or a dense shrub, but they also seek surface debris—such as stored roofing tins—or fallen buildings beneath which to thermoregulate. They prowl extensively during warm, gentle weather, and in hot weather they remain active until far into the night. They are particularly active during the spring breeding season, when males diligently follow the pheromone trails left by receptive females. Corn snakes may bite defensively but often do not.

**Habitat/Range** This is a snake of deciduous woodland edges, mixed woodlands, and pinelands. It occurs in meadows, in pastures, and on prairies. It can be abundant in roadside windbreaks of Australian pines or Brazilian pepper. It survives, seemingly with little effort, in agricultural areas, suburban rock piles, and city yards. It particularly favors infrequently used outbuildings, stone walls, trash heaps, hay and feed storage areas, or any other combination of habitat characteristics that would induce or channel the movement of healthy rodent populations. Corn snakes are agile climbers that can be found rather high in trees or at any level in limestone caves or caverns (but do not seem to go far into the caves). They may be seen in the rafters or crawlspaces of dwellings and barns; coiled quietly in low shrubs; or in greenhouses amidst the stored pots in nurseries. In other words, corn snakes are a survivor species that can be found almost anywhere in Florida, from the Lower Keys to Florida Caverns State Park in the northern panhandle and beyond. Juveniles seem more terrestrially inclined than the adults. North and west of Florida, corn snakes range from the Pine Barrens of New Jersey to western Tennessee and western Louisiana.

**Abundance** This is an abundant snake throughout most of its Florida range. The Lower Keys populations (see next account) are protected.

**Prey** Hatchlings often prefer tree frogs or small lizards over baby mice for their first few meals. Although a hungry adult may occasionally eat a lizard or amphibian, corn snakes are essentially rodent and bird eaters. Prior to being swallowed, the prey is killed by constriction.

**Reproduction** When food is abundant and its health is good, this oviparous snake may have one or two (rarely three) clutches of eggs annually. The eggs in each clutch may number between 5 and 15 (more in well-fed captives), with a tendency for the second and third clutches to contain fewer eggs than the first.

**Similar snakes** Some specimens of the red color phase of the mole kingsnake may look superficially like a corn snake. However, the kingsnake has a narrow head and an undivided anal plate.

**Comment** Corn snakes now have been bred extensively by the herpeto-cultural community for more than two decades. During this time, more than 40 aberrant, or designer, colors and patterns have been developed. These vary from simple albinistic specimens to caramel colors, butter yellows, and pie-balds, and from normal blotches to saddles and even stripes. Since snakes are legendary for their Houdini-like escapes, it is feasible that you could meet a roaming corn snake of virtually any color, either in or far out of the snake's normal range. Such a snake may be difficult to identify, but in most cases the telltale spearpoint will be visible on the top of the head.

ADDITIONAL FLORIDA COLOR VARIANTS

## 16. Corn Snake, Lower Keys Color Variant

A naturally occurring and variable corn snake color variant occurs on the Lower Florida Keys. The Lower Keys corn snakes are often shorter and proportionately more slender than the corn snakes of many mainland populations. From 2½ to 3½ feet in length is typical.

Because they often have a rosy coloration, the corn snakes of the Lower Keys were once called "rosy rat snakes" and given the scientific name of

*Elaphe guttata rosacea.* Veteran Keys researcher John Decker now has defined the following four color phases of corn snakes on the Lower Keys:

Rosy phase—pale rosy-red ground color and maroon to red saddles;
Olive—olive-tan to olive-brown ground color with maroon to red saddles;
Silver—silver-gray to gray ground color with maroon to red saddles;
Chocolate—brown ground color when juvenile, but maturing into a typical-appearing dark red on pale rosy-red corn snake.

These snakes seek seclusion in palm boots as well as in virtually any manner of surface debris. Gaudy when in the open, their color blends surprisingly well with much of the native, low-growing vegetation of the Keys. These corn snakes occur on the Lower Keys, in fields, on golf courses, in tidal wrack, and in gardens. Anoles, geckos, and other lizards seem to comprise the bulk of their prey. This snake is protected on the Lower Keys. Apparently only a single annual clutch of 4 to 10 eggs is laid.

### 17. Yellow Rat Snake
### *Pantherophis (Elaphe) obsoleta quadrivittata*

**Nonvenomous** This is a large and beautiful constrictor that varies in disposition by individual. While many specimens are easygoing, others will swing quickly into a striking "S" shape, with the anterior of their body raised well above the ground, and will strike savagely and repeatedly. Their jaws are strong, and their teeth can produce lacerations that may bleed freely. If bitten, the wound should be cleansed and dressed as a wound from any source would be.

**Size** This snake and its relatives are among the largest serpents of the United States. Specimens from 4½ to 5½ feet in length are considered average-sized adults. Individuals of more than 6 feet in length are not particularly uncommon, and the greatest recorded size is 7½ feet! Hatchlings measure about a foot in length.

**Identification** Adults of this powerful constrictor vary from pale yellow with four wide and well-defined dark stripes in Alachua County, Florida, to a true (and rather pretty) yellow with variably dark stripes in South Florida. (North of Florida, the color may be a dark-striped olive.) South of Lake Okeechobee—an area where the influence of the now uncommon Everglades rat snake still remains—the ground color may near orange, and the stripes may be muted. The tongue is dark (with a red base in the south), the eyes are yellow to orange, and the chin is largely white. The belly is pale yellow. The 27 rows of scales are weakly keeled, and the anal plate is divided.

Juveniles of the yellow rat snake are as variable in ground color as the adults. Northern specimens are dark gray with black dorsal blotches. Southernmost specimens are light gray with dark gray dorsal blotches. Juveniles of the Keys variant (see next account) usually have an orangish wash to the light areas and brown dorsal blotches.

**Behavior** Yellow rat snakes are agile and persistent climbers. However, in cold weather these snakes often bask in terrestrial situations or may thermoregulate by crawling beneath a piece of plyboard or roofing tin.

These snakes are often seen prowling on warm spring afternoons and evenings, and during hot weather they may remain active far into the night. They seem prompted to action by afternoon showers, especially in the spring.

**Habitat/Range** This is a snake of deciduous and mixed woodlands and of clearings that is often found in the proximity of human habitations. It particularly favors infrequently used outbuildings, stone walls, trash heaps, hay and feed storage areas, or any other combination of habitat characteristics that would induce or channel the movement of healthy rodent populations. Yellow rat snakes are adept at climbing and are often found rather high in trees, in the rafters or crawlspaces of dwellings and barns, or well up on faces of fissured escarpments. Juveniles seem more terrestrially inclined than the adults.

This snake ranges northward from the Upper Keys, through most of peninsular Florida, then northward along the coastal plain to central North Carolina.

**Abundance** Prior to the partial draining of the Kissimmee Prairie and the Everglades (respectively, north and south of Florida's Lake Okeechobee), the yellow rat snake was replaced in those drainages by the more colorful Everglades rat snake. However, with much of the area now composed of high, dry agricultural areas rather than sawgrass prairies, the yellow rat snake has encroached on both areas to become the dominant form. It remains a common snake throughout most of its range.

**Prey** Hatchling yellow rat snakes readily eat lizards and frogs as well as nestling rodents and birds. Adults, however, prefer endothermic prey such as rodents, lagomorphs (rabbits), and birds. These snakes are efficient hunters that often indulge in wait-and-ambush hunting techniques but that, when hungry, will actively search out prey animals.

**Reproduction** Clutches usually number between 8 and 18 eggs. More than 24 may be laid by a large, healthy female, and 32 eggs were laid by a large captive. Well-fed wild females from the southernmost areas of the range may double-clutch, at least in years when abundant prey allows the snakes to maintain good body weight. Incubation may vary between 56 and 70 days but is usually from 60 to 63 days.

**Similar snakes** There are few snakes with which the yellow rat snake could be confused. The Everglades rat snake is orange and has weakly defined stripes. Related rat snakes are discussed below.

**Comment** Yellow rat snakes have been bred extensively by the herpetocultural community for almost two decades. During this time, a dozen or more aberrant, or designer, colors and patterns have been developed. These vary from simple albinistic specimens to caramel colors and piebalds, and from normal striped examples to blotched or patternless rat snakes. Since snakes are escape artists, it is feasible that you could meet a yellow rat snake of virtually any color, either in or far out of the snake's normal range. Such snakes may be difficult to identify and may actually require the observations of a veteran herpetoculturist rather than a herpetologist.

ADDITIONAL FLORIDA COLOR VARIANTS,
INTERGRADES, AND SUBSPECIES

### 18. Yellow Rat Snake, Upper Keys Color Variant

A color variant of the yellow rat snake occurs on the southernmost peninsula and on the Upper Keys. This snake was once described as "Deckert's rat snake" and was afforded the scientific designation of *E. o. deckerti*. This snake has a rusty-orange ground color (some specimens have a silvery sheen overlaying the orange). It also has variably distinct dorsal saddles. Juveniles are patterned

similarly to but more precisely than the adults and tend to have both ground color and saddles more brown than orange. Like other rat snakes, this beautiful constrictor seems prompted to action by afternoon showers, especially in the spring. It occurs in the coastal mangrove strand as well as in the interior hardwood hammocks. It is considered one of the rarer snakes of the Upper Keys but is now being bred in captivity in increasing numbers. This rat snake is not known to exist on the Lower Keys.

## 19. Everglades Rat Snake
### *Pantherophis (Elaphe) obsoleta rossalleni*

This snake is the most intensely colored rat snake of North America. With the draining of the Everglades, this magnificent snake has been overwhelmed by the encroachment of the yellow rat snake, a race preferring drier habitats. Intergrades between the two races are now the norm over most of the Everglades rat snake's original range. Nonintergraded adults of the Everglades rat snake have an orange body color, deep-orange eyes, an orange chin, and a completely red tongue. The stripes are weakly defined. The belly is paler than the back but orange nonetheless. The 27 rows of scales are weakly keeled, and the anal plate is divided.

Juveniles of the Everglades rat snake are buffy-orange and have well-defined brownish dorsal saddles.

This snake inhabits the few remaining flooded sawgrass/marl prairies. Look for it in isolated hammocks, along canals, and in Glades-edge windbreaks. Stone piles, oolitic limestone outcroppings, heaps of vegetation, and trash heaps are also favored habitats. It is restricted in distribution to the Kissimmee Prairie and the Everglades of interior southern Florida.

## 20. Gray Rat Snake
### *Pantherophis (Elaphe) obsoleta spiloides*

The gray rat snake may be better known by its colloquial name of "white oak snake" than by its accepted common name of gray rat snake. Where the color of this impressive snake is not compromised by the genetic input of other rat

snake races, the ground color of the gray rat snake is just that—some shade of gray. The dorsal blotches are dark gray and often have a lighter center. There are often dark vertical markings along the edges of each upper labial scale and a dark diagonal line from rear of the eye to the corner of the mouth. The belly may be a lighter gray than the back and usually has a double row of small, darker markings. Some white may be visible interstitially, especially when the snake is distended with food or heavily gravid. Hatchlings have a gray ground coloration and dark brown blotches.

This is a snake of deciduous and mixed woodlands as well as of pinelands. It may be found in clearings, in the proximity of human habitations, in infrequently used outbuildings, in stone walls, in trash heaps, in barns, or wherever else there may be a concentration of rodents. Gray rat snakes are adept at climbing and are often found rather high in trees or in the rafters or crawlspaces of dwellings and barns. Juveniles seem more terrestrially inclined than the adults.

The range of the gray rat snake extends westward and northward from the Florida panhandle to western Mississippi and southern Illinois.

### 21. Gulf Hammock Rat Snake
*Pantherophis (Elaphe) obsoleta spiloides* x *P. (E.) o. quadrivittata*

As indicated by its scientific name, the Gulf Hammock rat snake is an intergrade of two subspecies. It was once thought to be a full subspecies and was designated as *E. o. williamsi*. This snake looks much like a light-colored gray rat snake (or, conversely, a dull-colored yellow rat snake), but it has dark stripes as well as dark dorsal blotches. The belly is tannish-gray and often bears a double row of dark spots. There are often dark vertical markings along the edges of each upper labial scale, and a diagonal postocular line runs from the back of the eye to the corner of the mouth. Some white may be visible interstitially, especially when the snake is distended with food or heavily gravid. Hatchlings have a gray ground coloration and dark brown blotches.

The range of this intergrade form is primarily in the vicinity of Florida's Gulf Hammock, but it extends from Crystal River to Steinhatchee, then northeastward to the Osceola National Forest.

## Milksnakes and Kingsnakes, Genus *Lampropeltis*

Three species of milksnakes and kingsnakes occur in Florida. Two of these have more than a single subspecies in the state. There are also intergrades and color variants to be considered.

The kingsnakes are rather closely allied to the rat snakes and pine snakes. Captives of all three genera have hybridized and produced viable babies.

The eastern representatives of the common kingsnake have 21 to 25 scale rows; the scales of the milksnakes are arranged in 19 to 23 rows; and those of the prairie kingsakes in 21 to 27 rows.

The scales of all members of this genus are smooth and appear shiny and polished. All species and subspecies have undivided anal plates.

The snakes of this genus are noted for their occasional ophiophagous (even cannibalistic) tendencies. Kingsnakes and milksnakes seem immune, or at least very resistant, to the venoms of the various venomous snakes with which they share their habitats.

The prairie and the common kingsnakes share dark ground colors, while the various milksnakes can be brilliantly colored.

Some of the milksnakes are remarkable mimics of the venomous coral snakes, but the ring sequences of the two snakes are arranged differently. The coral snakes of the United States have the traffic-light caution colors—yellow and red—touching. The harmless milksnakes have the two caution colors separated by black.

The prairie and eastern kingsnake groups may be seen by day in areas of open land, including pastures and agricultural areas, along canals, beneath surface debris in rural yards, and in woodland clearings. The secretive scarlet kingsnake is often associated with pine woodlands.

## 22. South Florida Mole Kingsnake
*Lampropeltis calligaster occipitolineata*

**Nonvenomous** Although it is not as prone to bite as some other kingsnakes and is entirely devoid of venom, the South Florida mole kingsnake *will* strike and bite if frightened.

**Size** Most of the specimens found have been between 18 and 30 inches in length. The South Florida mole kingsnake apparently seldom attains a length of more than 42 inches.

**Identification** This is a slender grayish snake with olive overtones. The 75 or more dark olive-gray to dark olive-green dorsal blotches are usually dark-edged. There are lateral blotches between the dorsal ones. A postorbital bar is present but may not be well defined. Hatchlings are silver-gray laterally, olive-tan dorsally, and have black dorsal and lateral spots. A series of dark lines *may* be present on the back of the head. The venter is pale and may be spotted or clouded (but is seldom strongly checkered) with dark pigment. The smooth scales are in 21 or 23 rows, and the anal plate is not divided.

**Behavior** Very little is known about the habits of this slender, fossorial snake. Most of the few specimens found have been taken from sandy roads in orange groves or while crossing paved roads on spring afternoons.

**Habitat/Range** This secretive kingsnake is known only from a very limited range in the Central Florida counties of Brevard, DeSoto, Glades, Hendry, and Okeechobee. It has been found in sandy grasslands and open woodlands but mostly in old citrus groves.

**Abundance** This snake actually avoided detection until about 1985 and was not officially described until 1987. In the ensuing two-and-a-half decades, only about 50 additional specimens have been found. But even with this paucity of specimens, it is not known with certainty whether the snake is truly uncommon or just very effectively secretive.

**Prey** Small rodents, nestling ground birds, amphibians, and other reptiles are all accepted by this kingsnake.

**Reproduction** From 3 to 8 eggs have been laid by captive females of this mole kingsnake. Nothing is known about its reproductive biology in the wild. Hatchlings are about 7 inches in length.

**Similar snakes** See the account for the mole kingsnake (below), to which this snake is closely related and very similar. Corn snakes have proportionately larger (and usually redder) dorsal blotches, weakly keeled dorsal scales, a divided anal plate, and a strongly checkered belly.

OTHER FLORIDA SUBSPECIES

### 23. Mole Kingsnake
*Lampropeltis calligaster rhombomaculata*

The more northerly mole kingsnake has a ground color that varies from gray through tan to reddish. The dorsal saddles—which can number up to 71—may be olive-brown to tan to reddish but most often have at least a vague reddish tinge. The belly is paler than the dorsal ground color and may be spotted or clouded (but is seldom strongly checkered) with dark pigment. There is usually only a single dark postorbital stripe.

This secretive snake may be found in areas of yielding, sandy soils—substrates in which it may burrow easily. Open woodlands—both mixed and of pine—pastures, meadows, and scrublands are among the habitats utilized. The primary range of this snake is to the west and north of Florida. To date, this snake has been found in two disjunct ranges in the Florida panhandle counties of Madison, Gulf, Calhoun, and Bay. It is possible that the range of the mole kingsnake is actually contiguous, and that the hiatus is the result of poor sampling techniques.

### 24. Florida Kingsnake
*Lampropeltis getula floridana*

**Nonvenomous** Although entirely without venom, the Florida kingsnake can be a feisty animal. Many will assume a striking "S" shape at the first signs of molestation, but others will bide their time and allow themselves to be held, pushing with their nose against a finger or arm, then deliberately opening their mouth, biting, and chewing. Cleanse and dress a nonvenomous snake bite as you would any other open wound.

**Size** Although 3½ to 4½ feet in length is the normal size of this snake, an occasional example may attain 5½ feet in length. Hatchlings are about 8 to 11 inches long.

**Identification** This is a variably colored race with a busy, but often muted, pattern. The crossbands usually number 40 or more. Each dorsal and lateral scale has a yellow(ish) base and a brown(ish) tip. Age-related lightening of color can be pronounced, especially in specimens from the light limestone substrates of extreme southern Florida. These lightest specimens were once called "Brooks kingsnakes" or "South Florida kingsnakes." Although the long-used scientific designation of *L. g. brooksi* is now officially invalid, sadly (and confusingly), Florida kingsnakes are still referred to in this manner by the herpetocultural community.

The sides may or may not be lighter than the back. We have often found fully adult males from southern Dade and Monroe Counties and western Collier and Lee Counties to be considerably lighter in color than are adult females from the same area. The smooth scales are usually in 23 rows; the anal plate is undivided.

Hatchlings have a well-defined pattern and are often suffused with orange on their sides.

**Behavior** This is a secretive snake that requires only a little recumbent vegetation to be fully camouflaged. Its brown (or yellow) and cream coloration blends so well with its chosen background that the snake is all but invisible. Among the many snakes known for their retiring habits, kingsnakes reign as champions. These snakes also burrow extensively and are adept at following the subterranean trails of mice and moles. The snakes may be surface-active during the lengthening days of spring and in early summer.

**Habitat/Range** Look for this large but secretive snake beneath human-generated surface debris (boards and roofing tins are particularly favored); along grassy, frog-laden canal banks; near old houses, trashpiles, dumps, and barns; and anyplace else that offers adequate cover and food. In defining the range of this kingsnake, we follow Blaney (1977). In its pure form, the Florida kingsnake ranges south along Florida's Gulf coast from Tampa Bay to the tip of the peninsula.

**Abundance** Although found over a fairly extensive range, the Florida king-snake today *seems* depleted in numbers. This may be because of its secretive behavior and propensity for burrowing and not because it is an actual rarity. When the hottest days of summer arrive, the Florida kingsnake spends more time below ground and is only infrequently seen.

The distribution and identification of the snake now known as *L. g. floridana* was changed by Blaney in a paper dated 1977. Previously the taxonomic designation was used for the very abundant kingsnakes that are now considered peninsular intergrades. As once defined, these were distributed across the Florida from central Collier County in the south to Marion County in the north. Now, however, the accepted range of *L. g. floridana* is from Tampa Bay southward to the tip of peninsular Florida, west of Lake Okeechobee. When one uses these boundaries, the subspecies appears to be in decline. This is especially so of populations of the lightest-colored examples found at the southernmost extreme of the range, where both habitat modifications and collecting for the pet trade are rampant.

**Prey** Kingsnakes in general have a remarkably varied diet. Frogs, toads, salamanders, lizards, other snakes (including venomous species), small mammals, and ground-dwelling birds are all eaten. Some populations of the Florida kingsnake prey preferentially on turtle eggs and baby turtles. Neonate kingsnakes also eat some invertebrates.

**Reproduction** A normal clutch contains from 4 to 15 eggs, but occasional clutches from large females may contain up to 20 eggs. When food supplies are adequate, a healthy captive female may double-clutch. Whether multiple clutches are produced in the wild is unknown. The egg count in the second clutch is often considerably smaller than the first.

**Similar snakes** With its shiny scales, rounded nose, yellowish brown ground color, and chain pattern, the Florida kingsnake would be easily confused only with the intergrade form discussed next. Use range as an identification tool. Other variants and more precisely patterned races are discussed below. See also the account for the California kingsnake on page 137.

OTHER FLORIDA COLOR VARIANTS AND SUBSPECIES

## 25. Eastern Kingsnake
### *Lampropeltis getula getula*

This snake is of rather standardized color and pattern. The ground color is black or very deep brown, and the chainlike pattern for which this subspecies of kingsnake has long been noted is white, off-white, or cream. There are usually between 30 and 40 dorsal saddles. The chain markings are usually narrow. The hatchlings of this snake may be washed with a variable suffusion of rose or orange. This usually disappears within a few shedding cycles. Like many other snakes, this kingsnake is often drawn by a proliferation of rodents or frogs to many habitats associated with humans. Look for it beneath human-generated surface debris (boards and roofing tins are particularly favored); near itinerant sawmills, old houses, trashpiles, dumps, and barns; along stone walls; and in other such areas. Eastern kingsnakes are also found along the edges of swamps, marshes, dikes, meadows, fields, and weedy ponds; along railroad and road shoulders; in stump holes and under fallen trees—often in sunny clearings—in both mixed and pinewoods.

This remarkably powerful constrictor is found across much of North Florida, and from there it ranges northward throughout most of the Atlantic seaboard states to the Pine Barrens of New Jersey.

## 26. Peninsula Kingsnake
### *Lampropeltis getula getula* x *L. g. floridana*

The peninsula kingsnake is an intergrade form. It is intermediate in appearance between the two parent races. This is the commonly seen pet-store kingsnake with the milk-chocolate to chocolate spots on a cream to butter-yellow ground color and a busy pattern. Juveniles are darker than the adults. Peninsula intergrade kingsnakes often retain much of the dark pigmentation and the relatively strong pattern of the hatchlings throughout their lives. As would be expected, those at the southern and western periphery of the range are often more like the Florida kingsnake in appearance than those from more interior areas of the range.

This is the most abundant form of kingsnake in Florida. It occurs along the pesticide- and fertilizer-ridden canals in the cattle ranches, cane fields, and sod fields of Central Florida. In these seemingly unhealthy habitats, not only do kingsnakes abound but so too do the amphibians and rodents on which they feed. The snakes (and their prey) are concentrated in the mazes of oolitic limestone that line the miles of drainage and irrigation canals in that region. The snakes thermoregulate on the ground surface during sunny but cold or cool weather, but they seem to become largely fossorial during the hottest days of summer. This is a snake of sandy open areas. As currently understood, the range of this intergrade form extends northward east of Lake Okeechobee from Broward to Citrus and Volusia Counties. A pocket of what are apparently intergrade kingsnakes of this parentage also occurs in the vicinity of the Osceola National Forest in northeastern Florida and immediately adjacent Georgia.

## 27. Apalachicola Lowland Kingsnake
### *Lampropeltis getula getula* x *Lampropeltis getula* subspecies

The variably colored and patterned kingsnake from the Apalachicola lowlands continues to be a taxonomic puzzle. We refer to it as the Apalachicola lowland kingsnake, *Lampropeltis getula* subspecies. The majority of the kingsnakes from Florida's Apalachicola lowlands are very different in appearance from the eastern kingsnakes to the west, north, and east of the valley. Over the years, these kingsnakes have been referred to as both "Goin's kingsnakes" and "blotched kingsnakes." They were once afforded the now-invalid subspecific status of *L. g. goini*. Typical patterns include such variations as a light spot on each lateral and dorsal scale, no crossbands, and a dark vertebral stripe; as described above but with broken horizontal bars on the flanks; as described above but lacking the flank markings and the vertebral stripe; light-spotted dark saddles (of variable intensity and definition), with white bars at least 4—and in some cases 8—scales wide. The result of the wider bands is fewer (20 to 25) dorsal saddles.

Hatchlings may be suffused with strawberry or orange, strongest laterally. This attractive color usually disappears within several shed cycles.

Studies have attempted to define the genetics of the kingsnakes in this population, but these studies have seemed to pose at least as many questions as they have answered. For the moment, we will continue to refer to these magnificent snakes as having uncertain parental affiliations. It does seem likely that they are an intergrade form, with the eastern kingsnake being a known parent species but with the second parent species remaining an enigma. This is a snake of sandy open pine and mixed hardwood areas that support a tangled and pervasive undergrowth. The habitat is typified by the presence of tiny ponds, swamplands, and drainage canals. These kingsnakes are occasionally seen in areas of tall grasses but seem more common where the undergrowth consists of cat briar and brambles. They range in the Apalachicola lowlands, between the Apalachicola and the Ochlockonee Rivers.

## 28. Scarlet Kingsnake
### *Lampropeltis triangulum elapsoides*

**Nonvenomous** Despite being a mimic of the venomous coral snake, the harmless scarlet kingsnake is easily differentiated. Red and yellow—the two traffic-light warning colors that touch on the North American venomous coral snakes—are separated by black on the scarlet kingsnake. In eastern North America, if the two caution colors do not touch, the snake is harmless. Although some scarlet kingsnakes may assume a striking "S" pose and defend  themselves furiously, other specimens may show no evidence of temper whatever. This snake and all other members of this genus are entirely harmless to humans.

**Size** This may be the smallest race of the milksnake. Most specimens found are between 14 and 18 inches in length. While the largest specimens are in the 27 to 29-inch range, any in the 20 to 24-inch range are considered huge. Hatchlings are a slender 5¾ inches long.

**Identification** The smooth scales of the scarlet kingsnake are arranged in 19 rows. The brilliant rings of red, black, and yellow (or white) completely encircle the body. The red and the yellow rings are separated by black rings. The nose is usually red. Pallid (pastel) individuals are occasionally encountered. Except for having the yellow replaced by white, scarlet kingsnake hatchlings are colored like the adults. The head is narrow; the snout is narrowly rounded. The anal plate is undivided.

**Behavior** Throughout its range, the scarlet kingsnake is associated with decomposing trees and stumps—usually pines. It may secrete itself behind loosened bark or, in drier weather, burrow well into decomposing logs and stumps. During the high water of spring, scarlet kingsnakes often ascend well up into dead but still standing pine trees and secrete themselves behind the loosened bark. In South Florida, they have been found in damp crotches of Australian pines, beneath layers of fallen needles.

This fossorial snake is well adapted both for burrowing and for following the burrows of other small snakes. It is occasionally found beneath rocks but seems to much prefer stumps, trunks, and human-generated debris.

**Habitat/Range** Scarlet kingsnakes are common to abundant in areas with suitable cover. They are often associated with rather well drained pinelands, but they occur in mixed woodlands as well. Besides using fallen trees, dead standing trees, and stumps with loosened bark, these gaily colored snakes utilize human-generated debris for cover. In South Florida, the habitat of this snake is often associated with stands of introduced Australian pines.

The scarlet kingsnake occurs throughout Florida, but its actual existence on the Lower Keys is questionable. Beyond Florida, this snake ranges from North Carolina to Tennessee and extreme eastern Louisiana.

**Abundance** Because it is so secretive, the scarlet kingsnake is often thought to be rare. In South Florida, we have seen up to eight in an evening. These burrowing snakes usually do not emerge from their hiding places until after dark. Warm spring rains encourage ground-surface movement. Then the snakes may be seen prowling the woodland floor, crossing roadways, or (in South Florida) ascending rough-barked trees.

**Prey** Lizards (especially skinks) and smaller snakes are eaten by scarlet kingsnakes. Occasionally frogs are also accepted. Hatchlings from South Florida will often readily accept greenhouse frogs in addition to ground skinks.

**Reproduction** This oviparous snake lays between 2 and 8 eggs. Eggs are laid in decomposing logs, sawdust piles, beneath moisture-retaining surface debris, or, more rarely, beneath the needles in the moisture-retaining crotches of Australian pines (South Florida). Hatching occurs after about 2 months of incubation.

**Similar snakes** The coral snake has the two traffic-light caution colors—red and yellow—touching. The coral snake also has a black nose. The scarlet snake has dorsal bands, not rings. Its belly is white.

## Pine Snakes, Genus *Pituophis*

The members of this genus are moderately large to large snakes with heavily keeled scales and the ability to constrict. All possess a rather belligerent nature. Thanks to a glottal modification, these snakes have the ability to hiss loudly. They also have a penchant for vibrating their tail. Pine snakes have proportionately narrow heads. The rostral scale—the scale on the tip of the snout—is protruding, strongly convex, and much higher than wide. The pine snakes have four prefrontal scales. The body scales are in 29 rows at midbody, and the anal plate is undivided.

These snakes are accomplished burrowers. They pursue their rodent prey (often pocket gophers) in their underground burrows. Underground chambers (often of the snake's own making) are used for egg deposition. All members of the genus are oviparous. Most clutches consist of relatively few, comparatively large eggs. Occasionally a very large clutch may be produced. Communal nesting is well documented in some species. As might be surmised, the hatchlings are also quite large, some exceeding 20 inches in length.

Pine snakes can climb, but they do not seem to do so often.

Despite having a very different appearance, the snakes of this genus are rather closely allied to the rat snakes and the kingsnakes. Captives of all three groups have been known to interbreed and produce fully viable young.

These secretive snakes are associated with sandy, yielding soils, often in the proximity of pocket gophers or moles.

## 29. Florida Pine Snake
### *Pituophis melanoleucus mugitus*

**Nonvenomous** It should be noted that the term *nonvenomous* in no way means nonbelligerent! In fact, some examples of these snakes are so defensive

that they call attention to themselves by hissing loudly and rattling their tail. Many of these
snakes form an "S" with the anterior third of
their body and strike savagely if closely approached. Care (and a snake hook) should be
used if it becomes necessary to handle a snake
of this type. A bite should be cleansed and have
antiseptic applied.

**Size** The Florida pine snake is one of the larg-
est of the eastern snakes. They often attain 5½ feet in length and have been
reliably measured at 7½ feet. Hatchlings are usually more than 18 inches long.
**Identification** Although it is usually a pallid snake, the Florida pine snake is of
variable color. The ground color may be nearly white, off-white, pale gray, or
yellowish. The dorsum is usually patterned with gray to brown blotches that
are of irregular outline and may contain some light-centered scales. The
saddles on the rear two-thirds of the body contrast most sharply and cleanly
with the ground coloration. Dark lateral blotching is usually at least faintly
indicated posteriorly.

The head has some dark patterning in the form of dark pigment at the
scale edges and sutures or tiny dots on the scales. A dark interorbital line may
be present. Labial scale sutures are usually dark. The venter is unpatterned
and white or off-white.

Occasional specimens are virtually patternless. The heavily keeled scales
are in 29 rows.

Hatchlings usually have a very light ground color and well-defined blotching.

The head is narrow; the rostral scale is noticeably enlarged; and the anal
plate is undivided.
**Behavior** Because they are so secretive, it is not yet known with certainty
whether the Florida pine snake is merely adept at remaining out of sight or is
truly rare. Of the large, constricting snakes of the eastern United States, the
pine snakes are unquestionably the most fossorial and are for the most part
poorly understood.

Air expelled from the lungs past a flap of tissue on the glottis produces a
loud, wheezy hiss. Pine snakes also create a loud whirring sound (often mistaken for the rattling buzz of a rattlesnake) by vibrating their strong tail in
dead leaves or grasses.

When encountering gophers or rats in the rodents' underground warrens—where lack of space prevents the use of constricting coils—pine snakes apparently forge past the rodents and pin them against the wall of their tunnel with a muscular arc of the snake's body.

**Habitat/Range** This is a species of the rapidly and well-drained sandy uplands and barrens. These snakes are nearly always in the proximity of or actually within pine or pine-oak woodlands. The Florida pine snake is partial to loose soils in which it may easily burrow, and it spends much of its time below ground.

This snake—which seems nowhere common—ranges throughout the northern four-fifths of Florida, immediately adjacent Alabama and southern Georgia, and southeastern South Carolina.

**Abundance** Because the Florida pine snake remains beneath the ground so persistently, it is difficult to arrive at accurate population statistics. It seems nowhere common. However, it seems a certainty that because of Florida's rampant population growth and habitat modifications, the Florida pine snake is less common today than it once was. Florida statutes designate that only a single specimen of Florida pine snake per person may be kept without a permit, but amelanistic (albino) specimens are specifically exempted from regulation.

**Prey** Although a variety of rodents, birds and their eggs, and rabbits are accepted, wherever the ranges of pocket gophers and the pine snake coincide, those burrowing rodents seem to be the favored prey species. Their large size at hatching enables even baby pine snakes freshly out of the egg to eat fair-sized mice and baby pocket gophers. Hatchlings are also known to eat lizards.

**Reproduction** Normally, Florida pine snakes produce from 4 to 12 (rarely to 16) eggs per clutch. Heavily gravid females of this impressive snake have an immense girth. Deposition occurs in side chambers off of a main burrow. The same nesting chamber may be used for years on end, and communal nestings are well documented. The burrow may be constructed in a sunny spot on a sandy embankment, sometimes beneath boards or logs. Heavily shaded areas are usually not utilized for egg deposition.

**Similar snakes** See the description of additional pine snake variants below. Hog-nosed snakes are short and stout and have a sharpened, upturned—not a bulbous—rostral scale. The various rat snakes have divided anal scales, weakly keeled body scales, and a more bluntly rounded snout. Milk and kingsnakes have smooth scales and no enlarged rostral scale.

ADDITIONAL FLORIDA INTERGRADES

## 30. Black Pine Snake x Florida Pine Snake
*Pituophis melanoleucus lodingi* x *P. m. mugitus*

A pine snake color variant of apparent intergrade status has been found on the western panhandle. This is the black pine snake x Florida pine snake. It is dark in color even when a juvenile. The ground color is lighter than the blotches, but adults are so dark that it is difficult to describe a pattern. The snake may be entirely black on its anterior half but will show some poorly defined dark-gray barring posteriorly. The snout and face may be orangish  with an overwash of black. The venter is dark but often somewhat lighter than the dorsum. The head of this burrowing snake is narrow, and the rostral scale is noticeably enlarged. Look for it in pine or pine-oak woodlands west of the Escambia River.

## Short-tailed Snakes, Genus *Stilosoma*

This species is a rarely seen, burrowing Florida endemic. Crowned snakes (*Tantilla*) comprise the preferred—and perhaps exclusive—food of the short-tailed snake. Captives have steadfastly refused tiny snakes of several other species but have ravenously eaten crowned snakes when offered. The short-tailed snake constricts its prey weakly.

The short-tailed snake is a small and extremely attenuate kingsnake relative. It occurs in well-drained, sandy pinelands on the central-western peninsula. Very little is known with certainty about the life history of this snake. These are excitable little snakes that vibrate their tail if startled and will hiss and strike when further annoyed. They are entirely nonvenomous.

## 31. Short-tailed Snake
*Stilosoma extenuatum*

**Nonvenomous** When frightened, this slender snake draws its neck into an "S" and strikes persistently. It also vibrates its tail, producing an audible sound when in dry grasses or leaves. The short-tailed snake is entirely harmless to humans.

**Size** Most (of the few) examples seen are 15 to 18 inches long. This snake occasionally attains two feet in length.

**Identification** This very slender (about the diameter of a lead pencil), small-headed, small-eyed snake is a relatively weak constrictor. It will coil around and partially immobilize its prey, but it does not seem to kill it prior to ingestion.

There are two color phases, both of which have a gray lateral ground color and darker lateral and vertebral spots. One phase also has a gray back, but the other has an orange color between the vertebral spots. The ground color of the dark spotted belly is also gray. The head is barely wider than the neck. The smooth scales are in 19 rows, and the anal plate is undivided.

**Behavior** Not much is known about the behavior of this snake. It is a persistent burrower. It may be induced to surface-activity when heavy rains saturate the soil, and occasionally it is seen above ground in the evening in midspring. Since this is breeding time for most Florida snakes, and many *Stilosoma* found above ground are males, we can speculate (perhaps entirely erroneously) that the prowling snakes are seeking (or following) the pheromone trails of potentially receptive females. This snake will hiss, strike, and bite in its defense.

**Habitat/Range** This snake burrows in the loose substrate of Florida's remaining sandhills. Perhaps its most important area of remaining range is the Ocala National Forest, but the short-tailed snake persists in unknown numbers from Tampa on the west coast and the Lake Wales Ridge in Florida's interior to Columbia County. The short-tailed snake is a Florida endemic.

**Abundance** This is a seldom seen and probably very rare snake that is fully protected by the state of Florida. In our several decades in Florida, we have found only four individuals, and of these only one was surface-active.

**Prey** Although it is often said that this snake will accept skinks and small smooth-scaled snakes in general as prey items, it is likely that the short-tailed snake preys *only* on the small black-headed snake, *Tantilla relicta*.

**Reproduction** Other than the fact that this snake is oviparous, producing elongate eggs, virtually nothing is known about its reproductive biology.

**Similar snakes** Juvenile racers, coachwhips, and rat snakes have a pattern of dorsal saddles, but those snakes are big-headed and big-eyed. Although the pattern of the short-tailed snake is echoed by the two races of mole kingsnakes, the extreme slenderness of the short-tailed snake should provide immediate positive identity.

## Water Snakes, Garter Snakes, and Allied Species, Subfamily Natricinae

There are in Florida six genera of natricine snakes. Besides the very typical and well-known water snakes and garter snakes, there are the specialized crayfish snakes, the secretive brown snakes and red-bellied snakes, the burrowing earth snakes, and the tiny water snake look-alikes, the swamp snakes.

Most of these snakes are associated in some manner with water—either they live in or over it, or their prey lives in it. The brown snakes, red-bellied snakes, and earth snakes are exceptions. They burrow in the earth, sometimes in surprisingly dry locations.

The snakes in this subfamily vary in size from a length of only about six inches to a heavy-bodied six feet. None is a powerful constrictor; indeed, precious few even attempt to coil around a prey animal when it is seized. The natricines of Florida feed upon ectothermic prey—fish, amphibians, or invertebrates.

Very few of these species are coveted by American herpetoculturists, but many species—especially the garter snakes—are favorites of European hobbyists.

Many natricines will bite viciously if carelessly restrained. A few are easily mistaken for the venomous cottonmouth. Use care when seeking and handling these snakes.

**Natricine husbandry** The Atlantic salt marsh snake is a regulated species that must not be collected. The crayfish snakes and swamp snakes do require aquatic situations in captivity, but if water conditions are not optimum, these snakes will quickly develop blister disease or other skin disorders. These specialized snakes require specialized care (including diet) and are best left to the experts.

The burrowing brown snakes, red-bellied snakes, and earth snakes can be difficult, but often they are not. House them in a small terrarium with a clean substrate of sand mixed with potting soil in which they can burrow, a piece of bark beneath which they can hide, a shallow dish of drinking water, and slugs (red-bellied snakes), slugs and worms (brown snakes), or worms (earth snakes) as a diet. These small snakes often thrive at an ambient temperature of from 75 to 80°F.

Many of the water snakes and garter snakes, however, are pretty, hardy, and easily kept. These members of the family all have very similar captive needs. All should be provided with the largest possible cage, a *dry* substrate (dry is important!), and one or more hide boxes. Cage tops (or doors) *must* be tight and lockable. These snakes do not require elevated perches or platforms, but water snakes may use them if they are provided. The water bowl should be large enough to allow the snake to soak. It especially may wish to do so when preparing to shed its skin. These snakes are usually not picky eaters. Most will readily eat frogs or minnows. Many hobbyists feel that goldfish contain so many internal parasites that they are not a good diet. If you feed these snakes frozen fish, a thiamin deficiency may occur. We prefer to use live bait-store minnows.

## American Water Snakes, Genus *Nerodia*

The American water snakes are, for the most part, rather large snakes that vary in disposition from moderately feisty to downright irascible. If restrained, they are almost always either ready to bite or to smear an unpleasant combination of musk, feces, and urates on their captor.

As with many snakes possessing a Duvernoy's gland, the saliva of water snakes can contain complex proteins that may prove mildly toxic to some persons. Occasional toxic reactions to the bites of closely allied genera are well documented.

All of the American water snakes are live-bearing, some having immense litters. For example, a large (just under 5-foot) female Florida green water snake was carrying more than 128 well-developed young when she was run over.

With 7 species (a total of 12 subspecies), Florida is generously endowed with snakes of the genus *Nerodia*. These vary in size from the hulking Florida green water snake to the comparatively diminutive salt marsh snakes. No matter the size, all are comparatively heavy-bodied, and heavily gravid females may look almost grotesque.

Sadly, many of these snakes are regularly mistaken for the venomous cottonmouth and killed. Water snakes often bask by day, even in fairly cold but sunny weather. They often choose as basking sites warmed concrete abutments, protruding rocks or snags, or limbs overhanging the water. Basking water snakes are wary and will often drop into the water and dive at the first sign of disturbance. They may surface rather quickly and may either scull slowly in place or swim parallel with the shore to assess the severity of the disturbance. If again frightened, they often submerge and remain below the surface for long periods.

Water snakes may be very active on warm, rainy, or humid spring and summer nights. During such times of peak activity, water snakes often cross roadways, where vehicles can take a terrible toll.

Water snakes have heavily keeled, rather dull scales and, in nearly all instances, a divided anal plate. However, the several races of the red-bellied water snake may occasionally have undivided anal plates.

The snakes of this genus are almost always found in the proximity of water. They are often seen by boaters on quiet, secluded waterways but may be present in incredible densities on flooded prairies and along canals.

## 32. Gulf Salt Marsh Snake
### *Nerodia clarkii clarkii*

**Nonvenomous** Although the water snakes are considered nonvenomous, they do have a complex series of enzymes in their saliva. Some persons have developed edema and inflammation after being bitten. We suggest that care be used when handling all natricine snakes.

**Size** Although large examples can near 3 feet in length, most are smaller. From 18 to 30 inches is the more usual size. Neonates average 9 inches in length.

**Identification** Unusual in a genus of primarily blotched or banded snakes, the Gulf salt marsh snake is prominently striped. There is very little ontogenetic change from neonate to fully adult snakes. The dorsal ground color of this snake is gray to olive. There are four wide, dark stripes (two dorsolateral and two lateral) running from nape to tail. The belly is reversed in color from that of the dorsum, being reddish with a central light line. The heavily keeled scales are in either 21 or 23 rows, and the anal plate is divided.

**Behavior** Although it will bite if carelessly restrained, the Gulf salt marsh snake is not as irascible as many other water snakes. As high tides flood the salt marshes, these snakes disperse, returning to the tidal creeks at low tide.

The snakes bask and forage during daylight hours in cool weather but become largely nocturnal during hot summer nights.

Salt marsh snakes often forage for fish trapped in tiny tide pools. It is speculated that salt marsh snakes seek refuge in the burrows of the crabs or crayfish that abound in salt marsh habitat. Many of the snakes have imperfect tails, perhaps the result of amputations by the clawed crustaceans.

**Habitat/Range** This interesting snake—and its two other races (all of which occur in Florida)—is at home in a habitat used by comparatively few reptiles. It occurs in tidally influenced brackish and saltwater habitats but seems most common in salt marshes.

The Gulf salt marsh snake ranges westward from the region of Florida's Cedar Key to just south of San Antonio Bay, Texas.

**Abundance** This common snake is wary and secretive, hence it is seldom seen.

**Prey** Fish such as top minnows and other small species form the bulk of the diet of the Gulf salt marsh snake. Crustaceans and an occasional amphibian are also eaten.

**Reproduction** These live-bearing snakes produce from 3 to more than 10 young. Parturition occurs in late summer or early autumn. The largest females produce the largest clutches but not necessarily the largest babies.

**Similar snakes** There are no other snakes on Florida's Gulf coast with a combination of four broad and strongly contrasting dorsal stripes and a dark belly with a light midventral stripe. However, see the accounts below for the related mangrove and Atlantic salt marsh snakes.

Additional Florida Subspecies

### 33. Mangrove Salt Marsh Snake
*Nerodia clarkii compressicauda*

The mangrove salt marsh snake can near 3 feet in length. This is the most variably colored of the three races of salt marsh snakes. Some may be strongly patterned, others may be virtually unicolored. To complicate identification even more, the mangrove salt marsh snake intergrades extensively with the Gulf salt marsh snake on Florida's Gulf coast and with the Atlantic salt marsh snake on the Caribbean coast.

The ground color of the mangrove salt marsh snake may be tan, rich russet, black, gray, or olive. The snakes with the darker ground colors are often blotched or banded with darker color. Occasionally they may be striped anteriorly and blotched posteriorly. The reddish and tan examples are banded when young and may retain vestiges of the bands as they grow, but they often become unicolored adults. The belly is often quite like the dorsum in color, but the belly is paler and usually lacks a well-defined pattern. Mangrove salt marsh snakes are adept at finding both seclusion and basking sites amidst the stilt-roots of mangroves. The snakes bask and forage during daylight hours in cool weather but are active long after nightfall during the hot nights of summer. Look for them in tidally influenced canals, marshes, and estuaries from Tampa Bay south to the Lower Keys, then northward on Florida's Caribbean coast to Cape Canaveral. Mangrove salt marsh snakes are wary, often swimming to safety long before they become visible to an observer.

## 34. Atlantic Salt Marsh Snake
*Nerodia clarkii taeniata*

The federally endangered Atlantic salt marsh snake is the smallest of Florida's water snakes. Its record size is only 23⅞ inches, and most examples seen are between 14 and 19 inches in length. Neonates average about 7 inches in length. This snake has a rather dark ground color and a darker, busy—but often not precisely defined—dorsal and lateral pattern. The Atlantic salt marsh snake is striped anteriorly and banded or blotched posteriorly. The dorsal ground color of this snake is gray to olive. The four anterior stripes (two dorsolateral and two lateral) may be barely darker than the ground color. The posterior lateral blotches are often the most prominent markings. The belly scutes are reddish, and each bears a yellowish midventral spot. These snakes disperse as high tides flood the salt marshes; forage as tides wane, trapping small fish in tide pools; and then return to tidal creeks at low tide. Diurnal during cool weather, they become largely nocturnal during the hot summer nights. The salt marsh snakes may seek refuge in the burrows of the crabs that abound in salt marsh habitat.

The Atlantic salt marsh snake has a very limited range. It may be found in its pure form only in a few tidal waterways of Volusia County. Intergrades between it and the mangrove salt marsh snake extend a county or two further southward.

### 35. Mississippi Green Water Snake
*Nerodia cyclopion*

**Nonvenomous** These are irascible snakes that will bite repeatedly when restrained. Although they are considered nonvenomous, we urge that you read the cautions and comments in the genus discussion.

**Size** This is the smaller of the two species of green water snakes in Florida. Adults vary in size between 20 and 30 inches, with occasional females (the larger sex) attaining 48 inches. Neonates measure about 7 inches in length.

**Identification** Simply stated, this is a dull-colored snake with a bad disposition. Although adults are often less contrastingly patterned than juveniles, the Mississippi green water snake does not undergo particularly extensive ontogenetic changes. Mud will often adhere to the keeled scales, making this snake appear even less colorful than it actually is. To see any pattern on adult snakes, it is often necessary to see the snake when it is either wet or, better yet, freshly shed.

The dorsal ground color is olive-brown to olive-green. There is usually at least a vestige of darker bands. These are best defined on the sides. The belly is yellowish to olive with a pattern of lighter spots or crescents. There are several scales (the suboculars) between the bottom of the eye and the upper lip scales (supralabials). The chin is often yellowish. The Mississippi green water snake has either 27 or 29 rows of strongly keeled scales. The anal scale is divided.

**Behavior** These snakes are so uncommon in Florida that notes should be made and shared with authorities when one is seen. In spring, when nights are still cool, Mississippi green water snakes bask in the open extensively. During the summer, when night temperatures are warmer, the snakes are able to more easily maintain a suitable body temperature and forage well into the night. In summer, more secluded basking sites are also apt to be used. These snakes may bask on sun-warmed road pavement after sundown, a habit that leads to the vehicular deaths of many.

**Habitat/Range** Although a common snake from Texas to Illinois, the Mississippi green water snake barely enters Florida. There it occurs only rarely and only in the vicinity of Escambia Bay.

To the west of Florida, it is abundant in open marshlands, along bayous, rivers, canals, rice fields, and creeks, and sometimes in ponds and lakes. Florida specimens inhabit similar biotopes.

**Abundance** Although a common snake elsewhere in its range, the Mississippi green water snake is rare in Florida.

**Prey** Fish are the most important food item, but amphibians are occasionally eaten.

**Reproduction** This live-bearing snake normally produces litters numbering from 8 to 24 neonates. Clutches are usually born in late summer, but occasional early fall birthings are noted.

**Similar snakes** The Florida green water snake lacks a belly pattern. Other water snakes (except the Florida green) lack the subocular scales. The cottonmouth has a strong facial pattern.

## 36. Red-bellied Water Snake
*Nerodia erythrogaster erythrogaster*

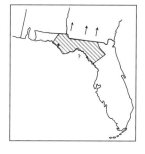

**Nonvenomous** When hard-pressed, these big natricines can be spectacularly feisty. They strike hard and bite readily. Although they are considered nonvenomous, some persons have reacted unfavorably to the bites of water snakes and garter snakes. We suggest that care be used when handling the snakes of this and related natricine genera.

**Size** Although females (the larger sex) often exceed 3½ feet in length (rarely, they may attain a length of 5 feet), they are usually somewhat smaller. Neonates average 10 inches in length.

**Identification** Considerable ontogenetic changes occur in this water snake. Neonates are prominently blotched or irregularly banded with blackish-brown on a gray ground color. The chin is yellowish. The belly is pale. As they mature, the dorsal and lateral patterns pale. Adult snakes are nearly uni-colored dark brown to blackish dorsally with a bright orange-red belly. The heavily keeled scales are in 19 to 23 rows at midbody. A great majority (but not all) of the specimens have divided anal plates. Mud and dust may adhere to the scales, obliterating the true colors.

In Holmes, Walton, Washington, and Bay Counties, where the ranges of the red-bellied water snakes and the yellow-bellied water snakes abut or over-lap, intergrades may have a curious yellowish-red venter.

**Behavior** These snakes occasionally wander far from water. They are, how-ever, most commonly seen swimming near springs or basking on river banks. The snakes are diurnally active during cool weather, but they may be crepus-cular or even largely nocturnal as the hot, muggy nights of a southern sum-mer take hold.

**Habitat/Range** Although these beautiful water snakes inhabit a multitude of aquatic habitats, in Florida they seem most often encountered along rivers, in cypress domes, and in open marshes. Ponds, sloughs, swamps, and oxbows are also favored. They may occasionally be encountered far from the nearest permanent water.

It would appear that the Florida range of this snake is not continuous. It occurs in Levy, Alachua, Gilchrist, Suwannee, Columbia, and Hamilton Counties, then again in Wakulla, Gadsden, Liberty, Jackson, Calhoun, Wash-ington, and Gulf Counties. It is not recorded from the "in-between" counties of Dixie, Lafayette, Madison, Jefferson, or Leon (but actually may occur there). North of Florida, the red-bellied water snake occurs in southeastern Alabama, over much of Georgia, then northward on the coastal plain to the central Delmarva peninsula.

**Abundance** This can be an abundant snake.

**Prey** Amphibians and fish are the most common prey items, but neonates also eat aquatic insects and perhaps crustaceans.

**Reproduction** These live-bearing snakes produce from 5 to more than 30 young. Parturition occurs in late summer or early autumn, sometimes when seasonal cooling is rather well advanced. The largest females produce the largest clutches but not necessarily the largest babies.

**Similar snakes** See the account below for the related yellow-bellied water snake. Red-bellied snakes are very much smaller and have 3 light spots behind the head that may coalesce into a pale collar and only 15 scale rows. Northern water snakes and queen snakes have a patterned belly with a pale ground color.

OTHER FLORIDA SUBSPECIES

## 37. Yellow-bellied Water Snake
*Nerodia erythrogaster flavigaster*

The yellow-bellied water snake is another of the water snakes that undergoes dramatic ontogenetic color changes. Neonates are prominently blotched or irregularly banded with blackish-brown on an olive-gray ground color. The chin is yellowish. The belly is pale. As they mature, the dorsal and lateral patterns pale. With adulthood, the snake assumes a nearly unicolored olive-black dorsum and a creamy-yellow to bright-yellow belly. The heavily keeled scales are in 19 to 23 rows at midbody. A great majority (but not all) of the specimens have divided anal plates.

Intergrades between the red-bellied water snake and the yellow-bellied water snake having yellowish-red bellies can occur in Holmes, Walton, Washington, and Bay Counties. In Florida, the yellow-bellied water snake is most often encountered along rivers, in cypress domes, and in open marshes. Ponds, sloughs, swamps, and oxbows are also favored. This is a snake of Florida's western panhandle. Look for it in appropriate habitat from Walton County westward. North and west of Florida, the yellow-bellied water snake ranges from central Georgia to Illinois and eastern Texas.

## 38. Banded Water Snake
*Nerodia fasciata fasciata*

**Nonvenomous** Despite being considered a nonvenomous snake, because some persons have reacted unfavorably to enzymes in the saliva when bitten by a water snake, we urge that care be used when handling these snakes or related genera.
**Size** Collectively, the three races of *N. fasciata* are

referred to as the southern water snakes. This and the Florida water snake (next account) occur in Florida; the broad-banded form as an intergrade with the banded—which approaches the Florida panhandle—is discussed on page 142. Although adult at between 24 and 40 inches in length, this snake may occasionally attain a full, heavy-bodied five feet. Neonates average about 9 1/2 inches in length.

**Identification** Both the ground color and the pattern of the banded water snake are variable. The ground color may be gray, tan, olive, or almost black. The pattern may be dark-olive, greenish-brown, old rose, or red. The bands may be outlined with darker pigment. There are not usually any dark lateral spots between the dark bands. Some banded water snakes are so dark that they may appear almost unicolored. If light areas are present, they will be on the lower sides. The belly is off-white to white and has an irregular pattern of darker (sometimes a quite bright red) pigment. The upper labial scales are usually outlined by dark pigment. A dark stripe may run from the back of the eye to the rear of the angle of the jaw. Neonates are more strongly patterned than most adults.

Although it is not known to occur in Florida, the range of the very pretty broad-banded water snake, *Nerodia fasciata confluens*—or at least an intergrade between this and the banded water snake—comes virtually to the westernmost tip of the Florida panhandle.

**Behavior** Although it is restricted closely to existing waterways during times of drought, when heavy rains flood pastures, depressions, and prairies, this water snake follows the changing delimitations. Banded water snakes are active by day in cool weather and by day and night in hot weather. These snakes bask on all manner of available sunning spots—fallen trees, projecting roots, branches of trees and shrubs that overhang the water, sloping banks, bridge abutments. If the habitat is accessible, the snakes will use it. Evening spring rains will often prompt vast numbers of banded water snakes to roam the proximity of their habitats, perhaps merely in an effort to disperse, perhaps in search for pheromone trails of a potentially receptive mate. When carelessly restrained, adult banded water snakes do not hesitate to bite. Babies are less apt to do so.

**Habitat/Range** The banded water snake occupies virtually every aquatic habitat except pure salt water. This race is restricted in distribution to the

Florida panhandle, adjacent Alabama, the southern half of Georgia, then northward along the coastal plain to northern North Carolina.

**Abundance** This is an abundant water snake—perhaps *the* most abundant water snake—throughout its range.

**Prey** Frogs and fishes are the preferred dietary items of this snake. Juveniles may eat aquatic invertebrates.

**Reproduction** From 5 to 25 (occasionally to 50) neonates are produced annually in late summer or very early autumn. Large females seem to produce the largest clutches.

**Similar snakes** See the accounts for the Florida water snake below and for the broad-banded water snake on page 142. Use range as a tool when attempting the identification of this snake. It can be confusingly similar to the midland water snake discussed on page 91.

OTHER FLORIDA SUBSPECIES

### 39. Florida Water Snake
### *Nerodia fasciata pictiventris*

This snake is the southern representative of this species. The Florida water snake occurs in almost every type of watery habitat on the Florida peninsula and the adjacent Okefenokee Swamp in Georgia. Both the ground color and the pattern of the Florida water snake are variable. The ground color may be gray, tan, olive, or almost black. The dark bands may be dark-olive, greenish-brown, old rose, or red. The bands may be outlined with  darker pigment. There may be dark spots on each side between the dark bands. Some snakes are so dark that they may appear almost a unicolored gray-black (especially when dry). If light areas are present, they will be on the lower sides. The belly is off-white to white and has an irregular pattern of darker (sometimes a quite bright red) pigment. The upper labial scales are usually outlined by dark pigment. A dark stripe may run from the back of the eye to the rear of the angle of the jaw. Neonates are more strongly patterned than most adults.

## 40. Florida Green Water Snake
*Nerodia floridana*

**Nonvenomous** Big, of sullen demeanor, the Florida green water snake is always ready to bite if carelessly restrained. Although these snakes are considered nonvenomous, a bite from any big snake is unpleasant. In addition, most of the natricines seem to have complex enzymes in their saliva that can cause edema and inflammation in some people. We urge that you read the cautions and comments in the genus discussion.

**Size** This is the larger and by far the more common of the two species of green water snakes in Florida. Adults vary in size between 3 and 4 feet in length, with occasional examples exceeding 6 feet. Neonates measure about 9 inches in length.

**Identification** This is marginally the largest and among the dullest-colored of Florida's water snakes. Adults are less contrastingly patterned than juveniles. Mud will often adhere to the keeled scales, making these snakes appear even less colorful than they actually are. To see any pattern on adult snakes, it is often necessary to see the snake when it is either wet or, better yet, freshly shed.

The dorsal ground color is olive-brown to olive-green. There is usually at least a vestige of darker bands. The belly is yellowish to olive and unpatterned except beneath the tail. There are several scales (the suboculars) between the bottom of the eye and the upper lip scales (supralabials). This characteristic is shared in Florida only with the closely related Mississippi green water snake. The chin is yellowish-green. The Florida green water snake has either 27 or 29 rows of strongly keeled scales. The anal scale is divided.

**Behavior** These big water snakes are often seen lying quietly at night along the edges of canals and flooded prairies. They are active by both day and night when the weather is hot but are largely diurnal during cool weather. In spring, when nights are still cool, Florida green water snakes bask in the open extensively. As temperatures increase and the snakes are able to more easily maintain a suitable body temperature, they choose more secluded basking sites and forage more. These snakes are particularly active during and following

evening rains in the spring and early summer. Immense numbers are killed by vehicles on canalside highways during the March to late May breeding season.
**Habitat/Range** This big snake can be abundant along rivers, canals, creeks, flooded prairies, and sometimes in ponds and lakes.

It is found virtually throughout Florida, in a narrow strip of adjacent Georgia, and in a curiously large and disjunct range in southeastern South Carolina.
**Abundance** When water levels are normal, this snake disperses widely and is commonly seen throughout most of its range. During years of drought, however, it is found only in the immediate proximity of standing permanent water.
**Prey** Fish are the most important food item, but amphibians are also eaten.
**Reproduction** This live-bearing snake normally produces litters numbering from 20 to 50 neonates, but a large female containing 128 partially developed babies was found dead on a Central Florida roadway. Clutches are usually born in the late summer, but occasional early fall birthings are noted.
**Similar snakes** The Mississippi green water snake has a prominent belly pattern. Other water snakes (except the Mississippi green) lack the subocular scales. The cottonmouth has a strong facial pattern.

## 41. Midland Water Snake
*Nerodia sipedon pleuralis*

**Nonvenomous** Although juvenile midland water snakes will often allow themselves to be handled without biting, this is not usually the case with adults. We are considering these snakes nonvenomous, but we urge that you read the cautions and comments in the genus discussion.
**Size** Sexually mature at between 2 and 3 feet in length (with females being the larger sex), occa-
sional examples of this variable snake top out at just under 5 feet in length. Neonates measure about 9¼ inches at birth.
**Identification** Although adults are often less brightly colored than juveniles, the midland water snake does not undergo particularly extensive ontogenetic changes. Mud will often adhere to the keeled scales, making these snakes appear even less colorful than they actually are. To fully appreciate the brilliance

and intricacy of the colors and patterns, it is often necessary to see the snake when it is either wet or, better yet, freshly shed.

The ground color of the midland water snake may be gray, buff, tan, brown, or reddish. The markings are usually much darker than the ground color, but this is not invariably so. The markings of the juveniles are often blackish, as may be those of some adults. On other examples, the markings may be reddish, with or without a darker border. Typically the anterior markings are in the form of rather regular, broad bands. At a point somewhat anterior to midbody, the banding becomes irregular or may change to a combination of dorsal saddles and lateral blotches (occasional specimens are regularly banded for their entire length). Tail bands may be regular or irregular. The belly is usually strongly patterned but may be sparsely so or virtually unpatterned except for a sparse to liberal dusting of dark dots. If markings are present, they are often in the form of two rows of irregular triangles, apex directed posteriorly. The midland water snake usually lacks a horizontal dark eye streak, has keeled scales in 21 to 25 scale rows, and a divided anal scute.

**Behavior** In spring, when nights are still cool, midland water snakes bask throughout most of the daylight hours, foraging occasionally. As temperatures increase with the onset of summer, the snakes are able to more easily maintain a suitable body temperature. Then they bask less and forage more. A snake seeking to bask will utilize almost any exposed, fairly dry, sunlit spot. Concrete or wooden bridge and dam abutments, rocks, beaver and muskrat lodges, exposed snags and limbs overhanging the water are but a few of the possibilities. Juvenile northern water snakes are less apt than adults to come ashore to bask, but if the only sunny spot happens to be a patch of exposed bank or shoreline, it will be fully utilized.

**Habitat/Range** Although of wide distribution to the west and north of Florida, within the Sunshine State the midland water snake has a rather limited distribution and precise habitat preference. Look for this snake along sandy creeks and rivers from Walton County westward. It seems most common in Escambia County, Florida's westernmost county.

Beyond Florida, this snake ranges from central southern North Carolina to eastern Missouri and Mississippi.

**Abundance** Although of limited distribution, the midland water snake can be quite abundant in pockets of suitable habitat.

**Prey** Amphibians and fish are the primary prey items, but various aquatic invertebrates are also eaten.

**Reproduction** This race of the northern water snake normally produces litters numbering from 12 to 36 neonates. Anecdotal accounts of larger clutches exist. Clutches are usually born in the late summer, but occasional early fall birthings are noted.

**Similar snakes** Although banded water snakes are equally variable in color, they usually have rather regular bands along their entire length and a dark, horizontal eye streak. The various races of the red-bellied water snake have unmarked bellies. Cottonmouths—the venomous species with which observers are wont to confuse the midland water snake—have a strongly patterned face.

## 42. Brown Water Snake
*Nerodia taxispilota*

**Nonvenomous** Big and feisty appropriately describes the brown water snake. Carelessly restrained examples will almost always bite. A bite from any big snake is unpleasant, and because of complex enzymes contained in their saliva, the bite from a water snake may cause edema and inflammation in some people. We urge that you handle all natricine snakes carefully.

**Size** The brown water snake is the second-largest water snake of Florida. It is exceeded in size only by the Florida green water snake. Adult female brown water snakes may occasionally attain 5½ feet in length. Males are usually substantially smaller than the adult females. Neonates are quite variable in size, measuring from about 8 inches to over a foot in length at birth.

**Identification** Fully adult females of this snake are of truly impressive size. Although most bear a rather well defined pattern, this may be nearly obliterated by mud on the scales. To see the pattern of an adult snake, it may be necessary to wet the animal. Patterns are very easily seen on freshly shed snakes. Juveniles are the most contrastingly patterned and brightly colored.

The dorsal ground color is dark tan to dark brown. A series of large, dark dorsal blotches is typical. Dark lateral spots, somewhat smaller than the dorsal markings, alternate with the latter from neck to tail. The belly is lighter than the dorsum. Each ventral scute bears two or three brown spots that form irregular lines. The chin is creamy brown to light brown. The strongly keeled scales of the brown water snake may vary in row count between 25 and 33. The anal scale is divided.

**Behavior** Boaters often see these big water snakes as they bask a few feet above the water in overhanging trees and shrubs. The snakes may also be encountered lying quietly on a floating log. Brown water snakes are active by both day and night when the weather is hot, but they are largely diurnal during cool weather. They are avid baskers throughout the year but may seek more secluded basking sites when the weather is very hot. Brown water snakes are occasionally quite active during and following evening rains in spring and early summer and may be seen crossing canalside roads at that time.

**Habitat/Range** This big snake can be abundant along rivers, canals, creeks, flooded prairies, and sometimes in ponds and lakes. It prefers habitats with ample dry, sunny basking sites. These may be logs or shrubs projecting over the water or may be water-edge rock piles and grassy banks.

The brown water snake is found throughout all of mainland Florida as well as in southern Alabama, most of Georgia, and northward along the coastal plain to southern Virginia.

**Abundance** The brown water snake is commonly seen when water levels are normally high; it may be localized and difficult to find when water levels have been reduced by drought.

**Prey** Fish and amphibians are the most important food item, but neonates may eat aquatic invertebrates.

**Reproduction** This live-bearing snake normally produces litters numbering from 12 to 28 neonates, but a large female may give birth to more than 40 young. Clutches are usually born in the late summer, but occasional early fall birthings are noted.

**Similar snakes** This is the water snake of Florida that is most commonly mistaken for the cottonmouth. However, although its head is much wider than its neck, the brown water snake lacks the strong facial pattern so typical of a cottonmouth.

## Crayfish Snakes and Queen Snakes, Genus *Regina*

Although the four species in this genus are considered prey specialists, preferentially feeding on crayfish, the snakes also consume the larvae of aquatic insects, with dragonfly larvae (naiads) figuring predominantly. The queen snake seems to prefer soft-shelled (freshly molted) crayfish, while the other species opportunistically devour either hard- or soft-shelled crayfish. Ongoing studies have recently disclosed that a component contained in the saliva of the glossy crayfish snake is toxic to crayfish, quickly rendering the crustaceans immobile and easily swallowed. Crayfish snakes often coil loosely around their prey, apparently in an effort to control the pinching of the crayfish's claws.

The dorsal scales of all four species are in 19 rows (midbody), and the anal plate is divided. Three of the four species have keeled scales; only the striped crayfish snake has smooth scales.

The striped and the glossy crayfish snakes are stout and shiny; the Graham's crayfish snake and the queen snake are rather slender, nonshiny species.

The striped crayfish snake diverges also in being almost entirely aquatic. While the other three are very tied to water, all—especially the queen snake—leave the water to bask and even seclude themselves beneath litter and rocks on the banks and shores of the ponds, streams, rivers, swamps, and marshes they inhabit.

Three of the four species occur in Florida, with only *R. grahamii* being extralimital.

## 43. Striped Crayfish Snake
### *Regina alleni*

**Nonvenomous** Although the saliva of this species quite apparently has at least minimal toxic qualities, it is not considered dangerous to humans. These snakes seldom try to bite when captured but may flail about with open mouth.

**Size** The striped crayfish snake is adult at a stout 15 to 20 inches in length. Occasional examples may exceed 2 feet in length by an inch or two.

**Identification** The shiny scales of the striped crayfish snake are precisely colored. The back and upper sides are olive-brown to dark brown. A one-scale-wide dark dorsolateral stripe is present on each, as is a vertebral stripe of similar width. The lower sides and belly are yellow, often with olive overtones. Two or three narrow dark stripes are present in the yellow field of the lower sides. The belly is often unmarked but may have a midventral row of small black dots. The smooth scales (the scales are feebly keeled above the vent) are in 19 rows. The anal plate is divided. The head is narrow and the supralabials are yellow.

**Behavior** This rather heavy-bodied snake does not usually protest capture with a great degree of energy. It may twist and thrash momentarily but does not usually attempt to bite. It may, however, smear musk and feces on its captor. It is most apt to be seen on warm, rainy spring and summer evenings.

**Habitat/Range** Look for this little snake amidst mats of water lettuce, hyacinths, pennywort, and other tangles of aquatic plants at the edges of slow creeks, rivers, lakes, ponds, swamps, canals, cypress heads, and flooded ditches. In such habitats, striped crayfish snakes forage for the crayfish (and occasionally other aquatic organisms) that make up their diet.

This snake ranges over all of peninsular Florida and on the eastern half of the panhandle. It also occurs in adjacent south-central Georgia.

**Abundance** Because of its secretive habits, the actual abundance of this snake is difficult to assess. A search of favorable habitats, either by day or night, will usually bring a specimen or two to light. However, their true abundance can be assessed when, on warm, rainy spring nights, dozens to hundreds of the snakes can be seen crossing roadways that transect suitable habitats.

**Prey** Crayfish and naiads are the primary prey items of this snake. Captive specimens have occasionally eaten tadpoles and mud-minnows.

**Reproduction** Heavily gravid females attain a proportionately immense girth. The clutch size usually consists of fewer than 12 neonates 6 to 8 inches long. Parturition occurs in mid- to late summer.

**Similar snakes** Garter snakes and the other species of crayfish snakes all have keeled dorsal scales.


## 44. Glossy Crayfish Snake
*Regina rigida rigida*

**Nonvenomous** Although the saliva of this species quite apparently has at least minimal toxic qualities, it is not considered dangerous to humans. The teeth of the glossy crayfish snake have been called stout and chisel-like (Dundee and Rossman 1989); they are hinged at the base, a characteristic that helps these snakes swallow crayfish. Occasional examples of the glossy crayfish snakes *may* bite when captured.

**Size** The glossy crayfish snake is adult at a stout 18 to 25 inches. Occasional examples may reach a length of 2½ feet. Neonates are 7 to 8 inches long.
**Identification** The three races of the glossy crayfish snake are difficult to differentiate. Where in the overall range of the species an example is found will be a useful identification tool. The dorsal coloration is a shiny dark olive-brown to brown, often

with thin, dark paravertebral and paler dorsolateral stripes weakly visible. The sides of the throat bear thin dark stripes. Placing the snake in water may make the striping more easily visible. The scales of the upper lip are yellow.

The belly is yellowish (darkest on old snakes) and bears two rows of bold, regularly sized semicircles.

The scales are keeled and in 19 rows. The anal plate is divided. Females of this race usually have fewer than 55 rows of subcaudal scales (the scales beneath the tail); males have fewer than 63 rows of subcaudals.
**Behavior** On land, this stout snake will often remain quietly in place when its cover is removed. It does not usually bite when handled but will smear musk and feces on its captor. The glossy crayfish snake is most active, or at least most apt to be seen, after dark.
**Habitat/Range** Streams, rivers, and their immediate environs are most favored by this snake, but they also occur in lakes, ponds, swamps, canals, and flooded ditches. In waterside habitats, glossy crayfish snakes seclude themselves in crayfish burrows and beneath logs, boards, or mats of vegetation. They also seek refuge in floating mats of hyacinths, water lettuce, and pennywort.

This race occurs in the northern third of the Florida peninsula, the eastern half of the panhandle, and follows the coastal plain northward to northern North Carolina. A disjunct population occurs in central-eastern Virginia.
**Abundance** Because of its secretive habits, the actual abundance of this snake is difficult to assess. A search of favorable habitats will usually bring a specimen or two to light, and fair numbers have been found on rainy spring and summer nights crossing roadways that traverse or parallel swamps or marshes or other bodies of water.
**Prey** Although well adapted physiologically to capture and eat crayfish, this snake also occasionally eats dragonfly naiads and other aquatic insects. Anecdotal reports have suggested that amphibians and fish may also be consumed.

**Reproduction** This is a live-bearing snake. Clutches of from 4 to 14 babies from 7 to 8 inches long are born in mid- to late summer. Heavily gravid females attain an immense girth.

**Similar snakes** Garter snakes are usually prominently striped and have undivided anal plates. The striped crayfish snake is visibly striped. The queen snake is less shiny, more slender, and has prominent lateral stripes.

Other Florida Subspecies

### 45. Gulf Crayfish Snake
*Regina rigida sinicola*

This snake is the westernmost race of the two forms of glossy snakes in Florida. It ranges westward from the Apalachicola lowlands to eastern Texas. The subspecies of this snake are difficult to differentiate. Where an example is found will be a useful identification tool. The dorsal coloration is a shiny dark olive-brown to brown, often with thin dark paravertebral and paler dorsolateral stripes weakly visible. Placing the snake in water may

make the striping more easily visible. There are no dark stripes on the sides of the throat. The scales of the upper lip are yellow.

The belly is yellowish (darkest on old snakes) and bears two rows of bold, regularly sized semicircles. Females have more than 54 rows of subcaudal scales; males have more than 62 rows.

This snake may be seen at water surface or crossing roadways on warm, rainy evenings.

### 46. Queen Snake
*Regina septemvittata*

**Nonvenomous** Although this snake will bite readily when carelessly restrained, it is not considered dangerous to humans.

**Size** Although often smaller, the queen snake can attain a slender 36 inches when adult. Neonates vary from 7 to 9 inches in length.

**Identification** The very aquatic queen snake is strongly bicolored. It varies from olive-tan to a very dark olive-brown dorsally and is yellow(ish) to russet ventrally. There is a wide cream to yellow lateral stripe on each side, and the upper lips are also yellow. There are two prominent dark, dotted lines near the center of the belly scutes and another dark line at the outer edges of the ventral scutes. Three thin—and often difficult to see—dark lines occur on the back. Placing the snake in water may make the dorsal striping more easily visible.

The dorsal and lateral scales are keeled and in 19 rows. The anal plate is divided.

**Behavior** When basking above the water, this slender snake is nervous and loath to allow close approach. When neared, it drops from its perch into the water and may either submerge or swim swiftly away along the surface. It may also be found beneath ground-surface debris at water's edge. When restrained, it will smear feces and a pungent musk on the hands of its captor.

**Habitat/Range** Streams, rivers, and their immediate environs are most favored by this snake. North of Florida, these snakes are associated with the rocky riparian areas, but in Florida—a largely rockless state—the queen snake occurs in cypress heads and along creeks and small rivers. It may often be seen sunning on shrubs or low in trees that overhang the water. When out of the water, the queen snake is very secretive, seeking seclusion beneath logs, boards, or mats of vegetation.

In Florida, this snake may be found in suitable waters from Liberty County west on the Florida panhandle. North of Florida, this is not a coastal plain species. It may be found in inland habitats northward to Pennsylvania, Wisconsin, and Mississippi. A large disjunct population occurs in northwestern Arkansas and immediately adjacent Missouri.

**Abundance** Because of its secretive habits, the actual abundance of this snake is difficult to assess. A search of favorable habitats will usually bring a specimen or two to light, and on rainy spring and summer nights, fair numbers have been found crossing roadways that traverse or parallel swamps or marshes or other bodies of water.

**Prey** Although the primary diet of this snake consists of freshly shed (soft-shelled) crayfish, the queen snake also occasionally eats aquatic worms and insects, amphibians, and fish.

**Reproduction** This is a live-bearing snake. Normally a clutch will range between 5 and 15 neonates, but occasionally clutches may number more than 24.

**Similar snakes** Garter snakes are usually prominently striped and have undivided anal plates. The striped crayfish snake is visibly striped; Graham's crayfish snake is less shiny, more slender, and has prominent lateral stripes.

## Swamp Snakes, Genus *Seminatrix*

This natricine genus contains only a single species, which has three subspecies. Two of these occur in Florida. All are small, primarily aquatic snakes. As the common name indicates, these snakes are dwellers of swampy, plant-choked, aquatic habitats and can be very common in some areas.

The swamp snake has smooth scales, but the scales of the first several rows above the ventral plates contain a light longitudinal line that appears superficially like a keel. The body scales are in 17 rows at midbody, and the anal plate is divided.

Although these snakes occasionally may be found beneath surface debris, such cover is almost invariably in the proximity of the snake's aquatic habitat. They have been found in some numbers in the lodges of roundtailed muskrats.

### 47. South Florida Swamp Snake
### *Seminatrix pygaea cyclas*

**Nonvenomous** These are mild-mannered little snakes that, even when newly captured, seldom, if ever, attempt to bite.

**Size** Adult at from 10 to 12 inches in length, the largest examples may reach a length of 19 inches. Neonates are just over 4 inches in length.

**Identification** In a color scheme shared by numerous snakes worldwide, the South Florida swamp snake is a plain, shiny black dorsally and a brilliant orange-red ventrally. Despite having smooth scales, the scales in the lowermost several rows have a faint, light, longitudinal midscale line that, at first glance, imparts the impression that they are keeled. A short black triangle is present in both anterior corners of each red ventral plate.

This subspecies is very similar in appearance to its more northerly races. Differentiating it from the North Florida swamp snake requires counting belly scales. The South Florida swamp snake has fewer than 118 belly scales, while the North Florida subspecies has between 118 and 124. Range will also help identify the races.

The head is narrow and elongate, but it is distinctly wider than the neck.

The scales are arranged in 17 rows, and the anal plate is divided.

**Behavior** Although they may wriggle energetically when captured, swamp snakes are very reluctant to bite. During droughts, when many ponds diminish in size, swamp snakes may seek temporary to rather long-term refuge in the burrows of crayfish.

**Habitat/Range** The South Florida swamp snake occurs in cypress heads, swamps, marshes, and in any other body of still or slowly moving, plant-choked water. Temporary ponds are often used by these snakes. Where water hyacinths still occur, their roots often offer refuge for considerable numbers of these snakes and for other aquatic organisms. Although most common in fresh waters, swamp snakes are also at home in waters with a considerable saline content. It may occasionally seclude itself in water-edge mats of vegetation, and it has been found burrowed deeply into sphagnum mats and beneath decomposing pondside vegetation. Although it is primarily a mainland species, a few have been found on barrier islands. Rainy nights induce overland movement, and numbers of these small snakes have been encountered crossing wet, lowland roadways that are bordered by canals or flooded ditches.

This subspecies ranges southward to the tip of peninsular Florida from the approximate latitude of Tampa Bay and Vero Beach.

**Abundance** Although so secretive that its presence may be unsuspected, the swamp snake can be common to abundant in suitable patches of habitat.

**Prey** Invertebrates such as aquatic worms and leeches, as well as tadpoles, salamanders (including dwarf sirens), and small fish, are the usual prey items.

**Reproduction** A live-bearing species, the South Florida swamp snake has clutches of up to 14 babies that are virtually identical in appearance to the adults. Heavily gravid females attain a comparatively immense girth.

**Similar snakes** The red-bellied snake has a lighter dorsum and keeled scales. Red-bellied water snakes also have keeled scales, and juveniles have prominent dorsal bands and a light belly; adults have an orange to orange-red belly and a russet dorsum.

### 48. North Florida Swamp Snake
*Seminatrix pygaea pygaea*

The North Florida swamp snake is very similar in appearance to the South Florida swamp snake, but this subspecies may have a short black bar at each outer edge of each red ventral plate. Positive identification of this race of swamp snake requires counting belly scales. The North Florida swamp snake has between 118 and 124 belly scales, while the South Florida race has fewer than 118. Range will also help identify the races. This swamp snake ranges northward from the approximate latitude of Tampa Bay and Vero Beach, westward through most of the panhandle to south central Alabama and eastern Georgia.


## Brown Snakes and Red-bellied Snakes, Genus *Storeria*

Three species of this natricine genus occur in the United States, and representatives of all three are found in Florida. In fact, Florida is the stronghold for one, the Florida brown snake, *Storeria victa*. Only recently *Storeria victa* has been removed from the umbrella of *S. dekayi* and afforded status as a full species. All species in this genus have a divided anal scute and keeled dorsal and lateral scales, and all species *usually* lack loreal scales, a scale present in many snakes on each side of the head between the preocular scales and the posterior nasal scale. Except for the Florida brown snake, *S. victa*—which, like the red-bellied snakes, has 15 scale rows—the brown snakes have 17 scale rows.

While the members of this genus seldom (if ever) bite when grasped, all readily void musk and smear feces and urates on their captor when grasped.

Open woodlands, backyards, marsh edges, and most habitats between these extremes are frequented by the snakes of this genus.

## 49. Marsh Brown Snake
### *Storeria dekayi limnetes*

**Nonvenomous** Like all other members of this natricine genus, the marsh brown snake is harmless to humans.

**Size** This subspecies of brown snake is sexually mature at from 8 to 12 inches in length, but it may occasionally near 16 inches in length.

**Identification** The various races of the brown snake can be very difficult to differentiate. Use range to assist in identification.

The marsh brown snake is of quite typical appearance. The dorsum may be a warm to dark brown, yellowish-brown, reddish-brown, or olive-brown. A broad, light vertebral stripe is often apparent. Regularly placed, paired dark dots are present along both sides of the light vertebral stripe. The interstitial skin is whitish and may be easily visible when the snake inflates or flattens itself in fright. The ventral coloration may vary from yellowish, through pale brown or whitish, to pinkish. Small dark dots may be present at the outermost extremes of the ventral scales. There is no dark labial barring. The crown of the head is darker than the body. The upper half of the temporal scale is dark; the lower half is light. The keeled body scales are in 17 rows. The anal plate is divided.

Neonates are very dark in overall color.

**Behavior** If surprised or frightened, the brown snake may either flatten or inflate its body (thus making the light interstitial skin visible), flatten the head, and strike repeatedly. It is capable of burrowing but prefers loose and rather well drained soils. The brown snake is far more apt to secrete itself beneath surface debris (discarded newspapers and cardboard, roofing tins, logs, even packed leaves) than to burrow. They are occasionally found behind the loose bark on decaying stumps.

Brown snakes may be surface-active on relatively warm spring nights. Since there is almost always a preponderance of males at such times, it is speculated that they are searching for females.

**Habitat/Range** Although a marsh and lowland dweller, this little snake is seldom found where conditions are actually wet. Rather, they find suitable microhabitat on levees, dikes, at marsh edge, and in other such slightly elevated areas. They also find areas of seclusion above the high-tide mark on seashores and barrier islands.

In Florida, this race of brown snake ranges westward to the Florida-Alabama state line from the vicinity of Pensacola. From there, the range continues along the Gulf coastal plain to the vicinity of San Antonio Bay on the Texas Gulf coast.

**Abundance** The marsh brown snake is not a common species in its limited Florida range, but it can be abundant farther to the west. A half-dozen specimens were found beneath a single piece of discarded cardboard at an I-10 rest stop in western coastal Mississippi.

Burgeoning human populations and other urban and suburban pressures, including the use of pesticides, have inevitably taken their tolls on the populations of other races of brown snake. It seems quite unlikely that the marsh brown snake has escaped these pressures unscathed.

**Prey** Earthworms and slugs are eagerly eaten, but it is likely that cutworms and other larval insects, salamanders, and other tiny vertebrates are also eaten.

**Reproduction** A 12-inch-long captive female marsh brown snake, gravid when collected, gave birth to 5 neonates that each measured about 3½ inches in length.

**Similar snakes** See the accounts for other brown snakes below and on page 107. The related red-bellied snakes closely resemble the brown snakes. However, red-bellied snakes lack the diagonal dark marking posterior to the eye and have a brilliant red-orange (rarely slate-gray or nearly black) venter. Smooth and rough earth snakes each have a loreal scale, a pointed nose, and may have the dorsum peppered with a dusting of black dots.

OTHER FLORIDA SUBSPECIES

## 50. Midland Brown Snake
### *Storeria dekayi wrightorum*

The ground color of the midland brown snake may vary from tan, through light brown to olive or reddish brown. A dorsolateral row of darker spots is present. Although it is often stated that the paired dark spots are connected dorsally by a dark line, this is not always the case. In truth, the subspecies of the brown snake are difficult to identify, and differentiating characteristics

may overlap broadly. This, of course, is particularly so in areas of intergradation. The crown of the head is normally darker than the body color, a light middorsal line may be present, and the venter may vary from cream to a very pale pinkish-white. A dark subocular spot makes the eye appear quite large. Larger dark temporal and nape spots are also present.

In Florida, the midland brown snake occurs in open but moisture-retaining woodlands and fields, meadow edges, grassy fencerows, and mulched gardens with stepping stones. From its range in Florida's central panhandle, Alabama, and Louisiana, this race of brown snake ranges northward to southern Michigan and northern Indiana.

## 51. Florida Red-bellied Snake
### *Storeria occipitomaculata obscura*

**Nonvenomous** This tiny snake is entirely harmless to humans.

**Size** This is the smallest of the three U.S. species of *Storeria*. Adults measure from 8 to 10 inches in length. Occasional individuals may attain a foot in length.

**Identification** The keeled scales of the Florida red-bellied snake are in 15 rows. The anal plate is divided.

The red-bellied snake is among the most beautifully colored of serpents. The dorsal coloration is variable. While tan to russet seem the most commonly seen colors, a dark gray ground may occasionally be seen. The belly is usually an intense orange-red, but gray- and black-bellied specimens have occasionally been found. A pale middorsal stripe *may* be present and *may* be separated from the lateral coloration by a thin darker line. If present, these markings are often most prominent anteriorly. Vague indications of a light lateral line are sometimes present, especially on specimens with a light dorsum.

Characteristically, there is a light collar behind the dark head. The collar is formed of three (usually contiguous) blotches. Occasionally the blotches may fail to touch each other (this is especially true of panhandle specimens). A light spot is present on the upper lip below and slightly to the rear (supra-labial scale 5) of each eye.

At birth, red-bellied snakes are darker and more obscurely marked than the adults.

**Behavior** This snake may flatten its body and head when threatened and may also hide its head in the center of its coils. In a strange and entirely enigmatic behavioral pattern, occasional specimens may draw the upper lips upward, exposing the teeth.

The red-bellied snake is reluctant to leave its cover by day. They are occasionally found moving on warm and rainy spring and early summer nights. Breeding may occur both in the autumn and spring, but spring breeding seems to dominate. It is possible that males found wandering in the spring are searching for females.

Parturition in the wild seems to occur between mid-June and August.

**Habitat/Range** The Florida red-bellied snake ranges northward from northern Florida to southern Arkansas and central Georgia. Rocks and logs in both wooded areas and at the edges of forest clearings, as well as backyard debris, provide cover for these tiny snakes. Since they do not seem to wander far, red-bellied snakes are most closely associated with areas that, while not wet, retain at least a bit of moisture.

**Abundance** Although Florida red-bellied snakes are widely distributed, we have not found this snake to be common in any given area. For example, although we provide ample cover for secretive snakes in our yard in Gainesville, Florida, we have found only six Florida red-bellied snakes in as many years—and three of these were found in a single year. So tiny and retiring is this species that it can hide from view beneath just a few blades of grass.

**Prey** The red-bellied snake is a slug specialist, and some specimens may refuse all other prey items. Reports exist of red-bellied snakes eating small snails that they have removed from their shells. Some examples will also accept earthworms as prey.

**Reproduction** From 2 to 6 babies seem to comprise a normal clutch. Parturition occurs during summer, and the newborns average 3½ inches in length. Breeding apparently occurs during both autumn and spring.

**Similar snakes** The much larger size and lack of nape and uncial spots will differentiate the red-bellied water snake from the diminutive red-bellied snake; juveniles of the red-bellied water snake have pale bellies and are strongly banded dorsally. The pinewoods snake has smooth scales and a white belly. Neither species of earth snake has a red-orange venter, and both have a sharply pointed snout.

## 52. Florida Brown Snake
### *Storeria victa*

**Nonvenomous** This is a tiny but feisty snake that is entirely harmless to humans.

**Size** This is one of the smaller brown snakes. Most examples found are between 8 and 10 inches in length, and 12 inches seems to be the maximum length.

**Identification** The keeled scales of this small snake are arranged in 15 rows. No apical pits are present. The anal plate is divided. The ground color may vary from tan, through various shades of brown, but often has olive overtones. Reddish-brown examples are not uncommon. A light vertebral stripe is usually quite evident, and a row of darker spots parallels each side of this. When the snake inflates its body to hiss, white interstitial spots become visible. The 15 rows of scales (as opposed to 17) differentiate this brown snake from others. The crown of the head is normally darker than the body color, a light collar is present, and the venter may vary from cream to a very pale pinkish-white. A dark subocular spot masks the outline of the eye.

**Behavior** When on the defensive, the Florida brown snake may hiss and either flatten or inflate the anterior of its body. It may strike repeatedly (often with mouth closed) at the source of annoyance. When grasped, this snake will writhe and energetically smear its cloacal contents on its captor.

**Habitat/Range** The habitat preferred by this snake is similar to that of others in the genus. Expect to see this snake in open but moisture-retaining wood-lands and fields, meadow edges, grassy fencerows, and moisture-retaining bottomlands. In such habitats, Florida brown snakes seek shelter beneath dis-carded human-generated debris as well as under fallen tree trunks and other naturally occurring cover. This snake prefers moist but not wet habitats.

The Florida brown snake ranges over most of peninsular Florida and southeastern Georgia. A disjunct population of threatened status is found on Florida's Lower Keys.

**Abundance** Although not uncommon, this secretive little snake is not frequently seen. Although almost always found beneath cover, warm evenings—especially warm rainy evenings—may occasionally prompt a spate of surface activity. It is possible that imported fire ants may be adversely impacting some populations of this snake.

**Prey** Slugs and earthworms are the primary dietary items of the Florida brown snake, but insects are occasionally accepted.

**Reproduction** The Florida brown snake is live-bearing (viviparous). Clutches of from 2 to 10 neonates that are 3½ inches long are produced.

**Similar snakes** See the accounts for the marsh brown snake and the midland brown snake (pages 103 and 104). Red-bellied snakes have strongly colored bellies. Pine woods snakes have smooth scales; crowned snakes have smooth scales and narrow, black heads; and earth snakes have narrow heads and a horizontal loreal scale.

## Ribbon Snakes and Garter Snakes, Genus *Thamnophis*

There are two species of this genus in Florida. The ribbon snake, *T. sauritus,* is represented by three races, and the garter snake, *T. sirtalis,* by two. The characteristics currently used to define the various races broadly overlap, sometimes rendering identification difficult. This is especially true in both the blue-striped ribbon snake and the blue-striped garter snake. Both melanism and albinism are known. The ribbon snakes are merely slender garter snake species with very precisely delineated patterns.

Ribbon snakes are usually reluctant to bite, but a large garter snake can prove a worthy antagonist. If grasped, all will smear musk and fecal material on their captor. As a part of the defense display, garter snakes will flatten and laterally expand their body. This not only makes them appear larger but displays the skin between the scales and often heightens color contrast.

Although garter snakes are considered nonvenomous snakes, the bites from some have caused adverse reactions in some people bitten. All should be handled with care.

In Florida, both species of *Thamnophis* have 19 rows of keeled scales. The anal plate is *usually* undivided.

The garter and ribbon snakes are quite closely allied to the water snakes. In fact, some researchers have suggested that the two groups should be consolidated into a single genus.

There are few habitats other than the densest woodland and the open oceans that are not utilized by one or more species of this genus.

## 53. Blue-striped Ribbon Snake
### *Thamnophis sauritus nitae*

**Nonvenomous** This snake is entirely harmless to humans and rarely, if ever, attempts to bite. **Size** This is a fairly small race of the eastern ribbon snake. Most examples seen are in the range of 20 to 24 inches, and a 30-inch specimen would be considered gargantuan. Neonates are about 6 inches long.
**Identification** Here semantics reign supreme; as all toads are frogs but not all frogs are toads, all ribbon snakes are garter snakes, but not all garter snakes are ribbon snakes. They are simply different species of the same genus.

The ribbon snakes are, for their length, more slender and precisely marked than the garter snakes. Ribbon snakes also have a proportionately longer tail than the garter snakes.

The ground coloration of the blue-striped ribbon snake is black or a very dark brown. The lateral stripes are well defined and vary in coloration from quite a bright blue to a bluish-white. The vertebral stripe is usually poorly defined, being only a shade or two lighter than the ground color for most of its length. If blue appears in the vertebral stripe, it will often be only as a short streak on the nape. There may be a light spot on the rear of both parietal scales. A light vertical marking is present immediately in front of each large eye.

The scales are keeled, in 19 rows, and the anal plate is undivided.
**Behavior** This is a shy but alert snake that will wriggle energetically in an attempt to escape if grasped. However, it seldom bites. Like most natricines, the blue-striped ribbon snake will smear copious amounts of pungent musk and fecal material on the hands of a captor. When moving slowly, this ribbon snake often carries its head well above ground level. In this, it seems more like a racer than a garter snake.

**Habitat/Range** This small ribbon snake is found along the edges of marshes (both brackish and fresh water), canals, creeks, swamps, and ponds. It is often seen thermoregulating in the evening on the warmth-retaining pavement of roadways.

The range of this ribbon snake is only along a narrow strip of Florida's Gulf Coast region from Hernando County north to the Apalachicola region of Wakulla County. However, specimens having a similar degree of blue in the striping have been found as far south as the Everglades and as far west as Escambia County.

**Abundance** In suitable habitat, this is a commonly seen serpent.

**Prey** Amphibians and small fish form the dietary components of the blue-striped ribbon snake.

**Reproduction** This live-bearing snake produces an annual litter of from 3 to about 10 babies. The neonates are like the adults in color but often have slightly paler stripes.

**Similar snakes** See the accounts for the peninsula and the eastern ribbon snakes below. Garter snakes have the lateral stripes on scale rows 2 and 3 and tend to be stockier and less precisely patterned. Striped crayfish snakes are dark with *light* stripes and have a mirror-finish to their smooth, shiny scales.

### Other Florida Subspecies

### 54. Peninsula Ribbon Snake
*Thamnophis sauritus sackenii*

This is the most common of Florida's three ribbon snake races. It is also the palest and often the least precisely marked. Although the ground coloration of the peninsula ribbon snake may be dark brown, it is usually considerably lighter—even tan upon occasion. The white to pale-yellow lateral stripes are usually reasonably well defined. The vertebral stripe can be of variable definition—being easily distinguished on some specimens and all but absent on others. The unmarked belly is off-white to pale yellow. A light vertical marking is present immediately in front of each large eye. Because of their dietary preferences, ribbon snakes are usually associated with damp areas at the edges of water sources. Ribbon snakes are often found along the edges of bogs, ponds, lakes, canals, wet ditches, swamps, and marshes. They glide quickly and gracefully amidst tangles of vegetation or may occasionally seek shelter beneath surface debris. The range of the peninsula ribbon snake extends northward from Florida's Lower Keys throughout the peninsula, to the eastern panhandle and to southeastern South Carolina. It is replaced in Florida's Big Bend area by the blue-striped ribbon snake.

## 55. Eastern Ribbon Snake
### *Thamnophis sauritus sauritus*

This snake is the most vividly and precisely marked of Florida's three ribbon snakes. Typically, the ground coloration of the eastern ribbon snake is olive-tan to dark brown. Both lateral stripes and the vertebral stripe are well defined and butter-yellow to greenish-yellow. The unmarked belly is often a pale yellowish-green. There may be a light spot on the rear of both parietal scales. A light vertical marking is present immediately in front of each large eye.

Although it is the most widely distributed of the various subspecies of the eastern ribbon snake, this subspecies occurs in Florida only on the western panhandle. Beyond Florida, it may be found northward to Indiana, Ohio, and southern Maine.

## 56. Blue-striped Garter Snake
### *Thamnophis sirtalis similis*

**Nonvenomous** When provoked or captured, many blue-striped garter snakes will coil, strike, and bite. Others may hide their head beneath their coils and rapidly vibrate the tail.

Although inflammation and some edema have been associated with the bites of some garter snakes, it is still considered a nonvenomous form. We urge that care be used when handling this snake.

**Size** This rather poorly defined race of the eastern garter snake is adult at from 18 to 28 inches in length. Rare individuals may near a length of 40 inches. Neonates are about 8 inches long.

**Identification** The ground color of this snake varies from dark brown to black. The stripes are bluish-white to bright blue. The lateral stripes, which are on scale rows 2 and 3, are well defined, but the vertebral stripe may be prominent to almost lacking. Vertical black markings are usually present on the rear of each supralabial scale. The belly is off-white to pale bluish-white.

The scales are keeled and in 19 rows, and the anal plate is undivided.

**Behavior** We have seen this snake basking in early spring mornings as the warming pavement is dissipating the last tendrils of fog; found it foraging in September amidst the emergent grasses of brackish marshes; and seen it actively crossing rainswept roadways late in October, long after darkness has fallen. In other words, the blue-striped garter snake is active throughout much of the year, throughout most of the day, and often far into the night.

**Habitat/Range** The blue-striped garter snake occurs along brackish marsh edges and in open woodlands along Florida's Gulf coast from Hernando County to the Apalachicola National Forest in Wakulla County. Although garter snakes having blue to bluish stripes may be found from the Everglades to Escambia County, these extralimital snakes often have a lighter ground color than the snakes designated as *T. s. similis.*

**Abundance** In years of abundant prey and normal rainfall, this is a commonly seen snake.

**Prey** While frogs seem to comprise the majority of the prey items, worms, small fish, and probably some insects are also accepted.

**Reproduction** Little is known about the life history and reproductive biology of this pretty snake. Captives have bred in both autumn and spring but more avidly so in the spring. A captive female gave birth in early September to 17 babies 7½ inches in length. The babies were very like the adult in appearance.

**Similar snakes** See the account for the eastern ribbon snake below. The blue-striped ribbon snake is far more slender, has an overall "neater" look, and lacks black vertical marks on the upper labial scales. Other races of the garter and ribbon snakes have yellow rather than blue striping.

OTHER FLORIDA SUBSPECIES

## 57. Eastern Garter Snake
### *Thamnophis sirtalis sirtalis*

The eastern garter snake varies in ground color from tan to olive and from black to orange. The pattern may consist of checkers or stripes or a combination of both and may be well defined or almost nonexistent. In other words, the snake is variable in its pattern. If stripes are present, the lateral stripes will be on scale rows 2 and 3. The belly is off-white to yellowish or yellow-green, usually with some evidence of paired black spots on the anterior edge of each ventral scute.

This snake is very tolerant of both excessive heat and moderate cold. In South Florida, it is active year round, but in northern Florida, the snake may be dormant during the passage of strong cold fronts. It is adept at finding cover in grasses and plant tangles, and it seeks shelter beneath surface debris during adverse weather or when preparing to shed its skin. It climbs well amidst tangles and vines but is not often seen far above the ground.

The snake may be encountered in wet or dry prairie habitats, in open mixed or hardwood woodlands, along creek and river edges, foraging in brackish and freshwater marshes, at swamp edge, along canals, sunning on roadways, and in almost any other Florida habitat. It can be found throughout Florida (except on the upper Gulf coast of the peninsula, where it is replaced by the blue-striped garter snake) as well as throughout virtually all of the United States east of eastern Texas and central Minnesota. It also occurs in southern Canada east of western Ontario. It gives birth to from 6 to 60 live babies in mid- to late summer. The neonates are about 7½ inches long and usually very like the adult in appearance.

## Earth Snakes, Genus *Virginia*

This genus contains two species of sharp-nosed burrowing snakes. They prefer areas of loose soil but are most often found beneath surface debris in barely moist woodland, woodland edges, and woodland clearings as well as beneath stepping stones in urban gardens.

Because preocular scales are absent, the horizontal loreal scale touches the anterior edge of the orbit. The body scales of the smooth earth snake are weakly keeled, at least posteriorly (use a hand lens to check), while the scales of the rough earth snake are rather prominently keeled. Scales may be in 15 or 17 rows. The anal plate is divided. Neither species of earth snake has prominent markings, but both may be finely peppered with tiny dark dots.

Areas of sandy, yielding soils are preferred by these secretive snakes.

### 58. Rough Earth Snake
### *Virginia striatula*

**Nonvenomous** This is a tiny snake that is best described by the single word *nondescript*. This snake seldom bites, instead making closed-mouthed feints or hiding its head in its coils. It is entirely harmless to humans.

**Size** Adult at 7 to 9 inches in length, only rarely does the eastern smooth earth snake attain 12 inches in length.

**Identification** The dorsal and lateral color of this pencil-sized snake in Florida is usually olive-gray, dark olive-green, or olive-brown. It may rarely be brown to almost tan and lack the olive overtones. The dorsal scales are noticeably keeled but very shiny nonetheless. The scales are in 17 rows. There are 5 upper labial scales. A horizontally oriented loreal scale is present. The venter is whitish to off-white. The neonates are often almost black in color.

**Behavior** The very sharp nose enables these small snakes to burrow quickly and efficiently through yielding soils. Because of their fossorial habits, sizable populations often go unnoticed. Turning surface debris following rains may turn up a fair number of these snakes.

**Habitat/Range** In Florida, the rough earth snake is a denizen of loamy pinelands and grassy verges. It seeks cover beneath natural and human-generated debris.

This species ranges northward and westward from Alachua County to eastern Texas, central Missouri, and southeastern Virginia.

**Abundance** Actual population statistics of the rough earth snake in Florida are unknown. It is found with some regularity beneath boards and roofing tins on deserted homesteads but is seldom seen during times of drought.

**Prey** The preferred prey of this small snake is earthworms. Anecdotal references to subterranean insects and slugs also being accepted as prey are numerous but seem largely unconfirmed.

**Reproduction** From 2 to 8 live 4-inch-long babies are born in the mid- to late summer. The neonates are darker and even drabber than the adults.

**Similar snakes** Eastern smooth earth snakes have smooth or very weakly keeled scales and a more bluntly rounded snout. Brown snakes have preocular scales but lack a loreal scale. They also have a rather bluntly rounded snout. Red-bellied snakes have red, orange, or, rarely, gray or black bellies. Worm snakes have the lowermost one or two rows of lateral scales and the belly pink, the scales in only 13 rows, and are not yet known to occur in Florida.

## 59. Eastern Smooth Earth Snake
### *Virginia valeriae valeriae*

**Nonvenomous** This is a tiny snake that is reluctant to bite, but when disturbed, it may either make numerous feints or hide its head beneath a body coil. It is entirely harmless to humans.

**Size** Adult at 7 to 9 inches in length, only rarely does the eastern smooth earth snake exceed 12 inches in length.

**Identification** Dorsally and laterally the eastern smooth earth snake may vary from gray to reddish. Its color often closely parallels the color of the soil on which it is found. The 15 rows of dorsal scales are *usually* smooth but may be very weakly keeled. There are 6 upper labial scales. The venter is whitish or may have pale greenish sheen. The anal plate is divided. Neonates are usually several shades darker than the adults.

**Behavior** Even where they are relatively common, eastern smooth earth snakes are so secretive that sizable populations often go unnoticed. Because these snakes burrow during drought, even diligent turning of surface debris in prime habitat then may disclose none. However, many may be found when turning the same debris following a heavy spring or summer rain. During rains these little snakes may even occasionally be encountered prowling above ground.

**Habitat/Range** Florida is a state of sandy, rapidly drained soils. This is especially so on the southern peninsula. In Florida, the eastern smooth earth snake is a denizen of grassy verges, railroad embankments, stream edges, and the edges of, or openings in, deciduous forests, where it dwells beneath human-generated debris, fallen trunks, and other such naturally occurring cover.

Except for a very few specimens that have come from Highlands County, Florida, this species ranges northward and westward from Alachua County to Ohio and New Jersey. Whether the Highlands County population is of natural origin is speculative, and its long-term viability is questionable.

**Abundance** Actual population statistics of the eastern smooth earth snake in Florida are unknown. Even in areas of suitable habitat, it does not appear to be particularly common (especially in the southernmost portion of its range).

**Prey** Although this small snake has been reported to eat slugs, cutworms, grubs, and other such insect larvae, its preferred food is earthworms.

**Reproduction** Eastern smooth earth snakes produce between 3 and 8 live young in the mid- to late summer. Neonates average 4 inches in length and are often darker and even drabber than the adults.

**Similar snakes** Rough earth snakes have noticeably keeled scales and a very sharp nose. Brown snakes have preocular scales but lack a loreal scale. They also have strongly keeled body scales and a rather bluntly rounded snout. Red-bellied snakes have red, orange, or, rarely, gray or black bellies. Worm snakes have the lowermost one or two rows of lateral scales and the belly pink, the scales in only 13 rows, and are not yet known to occur in Florida.

## Snakes with Unresolved Affinities

There are several genera of Florida snakes that have not yet been assigned to subfamilies by systematists. Among these are the tiny ring-necked snakes (considered natricines [water snake relatives] by some systematists); the aquatic rainbow snakes and mud snakes (once thought to be xenodontines [currently a catchall subfamily of mostly neotropical snakes]); and those champion bluffers, the hog-nosed snakes (also often considered a xenodontine species). Additional research may show that these subfamilial designations are correct, but it seems more likely that it will be found that the subfamilial affiliations of these snakes lie elsewhere.

**Husbandry** The secretive ring-necked snakes can be difficult captives. Give them a small terrarium with a clean substrate of sand mixed with potting soil (barely moistened on the bottom layers) in which they can burrow; a piece of bark beneath which they can hide; a shallow dish of drinking water; and slugs, tiny frogs (such as greenhouse frogs), or tiny lizards (especially ground skinks) to eat. These small snakes often thrive at an ambient temperature of from 75 to 85°F.

The mud-eel- and true-eel-eating mud snakes and rainbow snakes are very difficult to keep. They should not be collected.

The hog-nosed snakes are interesting, hardy, and—if properly fed—easily kept. They should be provided with a cage of moderate size, one or more hide boxes, a water bowl, and a toad diet. Cage tops (or doors) *must* be tight and latchable. These snakes do not require elevated perches or platforms. The water bowl need be only large enough for drinking. If toads are offered, these snakes are usually not picky eaters. Some hog-nosed snakes have been acclimated to a diet of pinky mice, but abbreviated life spans seem the norm for eastern or southern hog-nosed snakes so fed. A natural diet seems much better for these snakes.

## Ring-necked Snakes, Genus *Diadophis*

This genus, restricted to the United States, Canada, and northern Mexico, contains only a single well subspeciated species. With only two exceptions in the United States, the members of this group are easily identified to genus by their brilliant orange to orange-red neck rings. The two exceptions are the Key ring-necked snake, *Diadophis punctatus acricus,* of Florida's Big Pine Key, and the regal ring-necked snake, *D. p. regalis,* of the U.S. Southwest and northern Mexico. On both subspecies, the neck ring may be muted or lacking entirely. Depending on subspecies, the eastern members of this genus of bur-rowing snakes may be denizens of woodlands, plains, prairies, or even back-yards.

When startled, subspecies having bright red-orange subcaudal color will coil the tail tightly and elevate it. It is thought that this aposematic coloration may indicate to predators a degree of unpalatability. Certainly some preda-tors have been known to eat and then regurgitate ring-necked snakes or to bite and then release the snakes, wiping their mouth against grasses or sand as if trying to rid themselves of an unpleasant taste. However, other predators—coral snakes among them—readily eat ring-necked snakes with no sign of distress.

Only two races of this snake, the Key and the southern ring-necked snakes, are found in Florida. A third race, the Mississippi ring-necked snake, is a pe-ripheral form.

In Florida, expect to encounter ring-necked snakes beneath surface debris (especially boards and flat rocks) in areas of easily burrowed soils. Yards, gar-dens, and vacant lots are favored habitats.

## 60. Key Ring-necked Snake
### *Diadophis punctatus acricus*

**Nonvenomous** Entirely harmless to humans, the ring-necked snakes do have toxic saliva to aid them in overcoming and, probably, predigesting prey.

**Size** At an adult size of about 10 inches, this is one of the smaller races of this wide-flung snake spe-cies. One tiny example, found beneath a piece of limestone on Big Pine Key, was only 3¼ inches in length.

**Identification** The dorsal ground color of this rare and protected snake is a light slate-gray to mid-gray. The smooth dorsal scales have a satiny luster. The venter is yellow to orange and lacks the black central spots of the southern ring-necked snake. However, the gray of the sides encroaches on the outer edge of each ventral scute. The tail is bright red-orange and is coiled and writhed when the snake is frightened. The neck ring is absent or pale; if present, it is usually broken vertebrally. The color of the few hatchlings known has been paler than the color of the adults. The scales are in 15 rows, and the anal plate is divided.

**Behavior** Like other ring-necked snakes, the Key ring-necked snake leads a secretive life and may be easily overlooked. These snakes are adept at remaining hidden beneath surface shingle and in the fissures of the limestone bedrock.

This race corkscrews the brightly colored tail as a defense mechanism. A captured Key ring-necked snake seldom bites but readily voids feces, urates, and musk on its captor.

**Habitat/Range** The primary habitat of this tiny snake seems to be beneath the surface limestone flakes in clearings and on the margins of hammocks in the pine-palmetto scrubland. It is known inhabit Florida's Big Pine Key, as well as surrounding keys.

**Abundance** This is a very secretive snake. Within its limited range, it seems to be very uncommon. It is legally protected in Florida.

**Prey** John Decker, a Florida herpetologist who has studied the Keys' herpetofauna extensively, has declared that the tiny, introduced greenhouse frog has become the primary prey item of the Key ring-necked snake. These snakes are also known to eat slugs and tiny sphaerodactyline geckos; they may feed opportunistically on other invertebrates.

**Reproduction** In keeping with its small size, the Key ring-necked snake seems to have very small clutches of very small eggs. A 9-inch-long female found dead on the access road to No Name Key contained two identifiable ova. The only other reported clutch is of 3 eggs.

**Similar snakes** See accounts for related ring-necked snakes below. Brown snakes have a whitish collar, a pinkish belly, and keeled scales.

OTHER FLORIDA SUBSPECIES

## 61. Southern Ring-necked Snake
*Diadophis punctatus punctatus*

This snake is the most common race in Florida. The dorsal ground color of this common snake is a light slate-gray to mid-gray. The smooth dorsal scales

have a satiny luster. The venter is yellow to orange. Each ventral plate bears a large, black,
central half-circle. The tail is bright red-orange and is coiled and writhed when the snake
is frightened. The neck-ring is well-defined
and is usually broken vertebrally. This race
commonly attains a length of from 10 to 14
inches, but it rarely may near 19 inches in
length. Southern ring-necked snakes are present in backyards, old fields, pastures, open

woodlands, and myriad other habitats. They gain shelter beneath all manner
of surface debris, both natural and human-generated. We have often found
fair numbers of this snake behind the loose bark on long-dead but still-stand-
ing pines.

The southern ring-necked snake is found throughout most of Florida except the lower Keys.

The Florida panhandle from the Apalachicola lowlands westward appears
to be an intergrade zone. Some examples from that region have the large ventral spots of the southern ring-necked snake, while others bear the tiny, paired
ventral spots of the Mississippi ring-necked snake. The southern ring-necked
snake ranges northward from Florida in the coastal plain and piedmont provinces of the Atlantic states to southeastern Virginia.

## Mud Snakes and Rainbow Snakes, Genus *Farancia*

The two species in this genus are specialized snakes that occur in swampy to
aquatic situations. When adult, both are specialist feeders on attenuate prey
items—salamanders in the case of the mud snake, and eels in the case of the
rainbow snake. Both species of this genus are red and black in coloration; the
mud snake is banded, and the rainbow snake is striped.

These snakes are of moderately heavy girth, with heavy necks and rather
small heads. The tail terminates in a spinelike tip. The shiny scales are in 19
rows; the anal plate is *usually* divided. Females of both species can attain more
than 5 feet in length. Males are usually noticeably smaller. Females either dig
or enlarge existing cavities or burrows in the soil—often beneath vegetative

debris—for the large clutch of eggs. Females of both the mud snake and rainbow snake often remain with their clutches during incubation.

This snake is associated with aquatic habitats and their proximities.

## 62. Eastern Mud Snake
### *Farancia abacura abacura*

**Nonvenomous** Although large, this snake cannot usually be induced to bite.

**Size** Most of the mud snakes seen today range from about 2 to 4½ feet. In bygone decades, it was not uncommon to find females six feet long. The record size is 81½ inches. Hatchlings are about 8½ inches in length.

**Identification** This is a robust, smooth-scaled snake with a small head and a tail tipped with a sharp spine. It is one of the species from which the hoop-snake myth started. This myth credits the snake with the ability to take its tail-tip in its mouth and to travel by rolling like a hoop.

The dorsal color is black. The venter (belly) is pink to red (occasionally white), blotched liberally with black. The red or white coloration extends up the sides in 53 or more easily visible triangles. The chin is yellow to pale red (or white) and is spotted with black. Hatchlings are often brighter than the adults, and in some cases the light markings may actually extend upward across the back to form rings.

**Behavior** This is a mild-mannered snake that can be handled without worrying about being bitten. Mud snakes are aquatic, secretive, and spend much of their time during the daylight hours burrowed well out of sight. At night they emerge from the mud to hunt for the aquatic salamanders on which they feed. At that time they may also search for mates. Afternoon and evening showers coupled with low barometric pressure often induce these snakes to move overland from one water source to another.

**Habitat/Range** Swamps, marshes, flooded prairies, shallow lakes (and the edges of deeper lakes), impoundments, canals, and many other aquatic habitats are populated by these water-dwelling snakes. They can be very common amidst and among patches of emergent and floating vegetation. Babies are often found in the dangling root systems of water hyacinths, water lettuce, and pennywort. When not secluded in patches of aquatic plants, mud snakes are often burrowed into the substrate from which they derived their name—mud.

The eastern mud snake is found throughout Florida except for the Keys and the western panhandle. In the western panhandle, intergrades between this race and the western mud snake occur. Outside of Florida, the eastern mud snake can be found along the Atlanta coastal plain from the vicinity of the Great Dismal Swamp (southeastern Virginia) southward.

**Abundance** The eastern mud snake is one of the most secretive but common snakes in Florida's waterways.

**Prey** Although hatchlings may occasionally eat tadpoles as well as dwarf sirens, adults are specialized feeders on the aquatic salamanders known as sirens and amphiumas.

**Reproduction** This is a fecund, oviparous snake. Average clutches number between 25 and 50 eggs. However, 65 to 100 eggs have been reported in single clutches on numerous occasions. The female mud snake often remains with her clutch throughout the approximately 60-day incubation process.

**Similar snakes** Only the western mud snake approaches this snake in color, but the two rainbow snakes have very similar forms. The red bars on the body of the eastern mud snake are in the form of triangles, while those of the western mud snake have flat or rounded tops. The rainbow snakes have a distinct lineate pattern.


OTHER FLORIDA SUBSPECIES

### 63. Western Mud Snake
*Farancia abacura reinwardtii*

The western mud snake replaces the eastern race in the extreme western Florida panhandle. It is slightly smaller than its eastern counterparts, topping out at 74 inches. The only difference in appearance between this and the eastern mud snake is in the shape and number of the light markings. The western mud snake has 52 or fewer light lateral markings with rounded or flat tops (as compared with the 53 or more triangular markings of the eastern race). The chin is yellow to pale red and is spotted with black. This race is uncommon in Florida but abundant elsewhere in its range.

## 64. Common Rainbow Snake
### *Farancia erytrogramma erytrogramma*

**Nonvenomous** This is another big, nonvenomous, nonbiting snake.

**Size** Common rainbow snakes between 22 and 42 inches in length are often seen. Those that measure 48 inches or more seem less common. The record size is 66 inches. Hatchlings are about 9 inches in length.

**Identification** This is a remarkably beautiful snake. The smooth scales of the back are black with three red lines. Ventrolaterally the belly is yellowish with some red interstitially (the skin between the scales). The ventral scutes are red with a line of black spots along each outer edge.

**Behavior** This is an extremely secretive, aquatic snake. It spends the daylight hours burrowed well out of sight in the mud at marsh or spring edge. At night it emerges from the mud to hunt for eels, its sole prey. It may move overland or search for mates on warm, rainy spring evenings.

**Habitat/Range** These snakes are at home in spring runs, at river edge, in shallow marshes (both fresh water and tidally influenced), and in cypress heads. Once common, they may no longer be so, but with a snake as secretive as this, it is difficult to arrive at true population statistics.

This beautiful snake is found over much of northern Florida. Disjunct populations may still exist in Pasco and Pinellas Counties, but specimens from these areas have not been seen in some time. The common rainbow snake also ranges southward and westward along the coastal plain from southern Maryland to eastern Louisiana.

**Abundance** The common rainbow snake seems now to be an uncommon species in Florida. It is more abundant in the tidal marshes in eastern Georgia.

**Prey** Although hatchlings may occasionally eat tadpoles as well as dwarf sirens, adults are specialized feeders on eels of the genus *Anguilla.*

**Reproduction** Average clutches number between 20 and 35 eggs. However as few as 10 to more than 50 have been recorded. Although it has often been noted that females remain with their clutches, they were not present on either of the two clutches that we have found.

**Similar snakes** Except for the very rare South Florida rainbow snake (see next account), no other snake species even vaguely resembles the rainbow snake.

Other Florida Subspecies

### 65. South Florida Rainbow Snake
*Farancia erytrogramma seminola*

This snake is Florida's rarest snake. Three specimens were found five decades ago (1952) by Florida herpetologist Wilfred T. Neill in Fisheating Creek, a heavily vegetated mud-bottomed creek on the west side of Lake Okeechobee. Despite extensive searching, the snake has not been found since then. If this aquatic snake still exists, it has proven admirably that it is extremely secretive and rare.

Very like the more common nominate form, the South Florida rainbow snake is somewhat less colorful. The dorsum is black with three prominent red lines. The ventrolateral color is largely black (some yellow and red may be visible). The ventral scutes are red with a line of large black spots along each outer edge. The preserved specimen photographed for this book is in the collection of the Florida Museum of Natural History. No living specimens were available.

## Hog-nosed Snakes, Genus *Heterodon*

Among the greatest character actors of snakedom, the hog-nosed snakes, when distressed, huff, puff, writhe, and bluff. They spread a hood, flatten their head, may strike, and when all else fails, they writhe some more, open their mouths, loll their tongues out to the fullest extent, roll onto their backs, and play possum. If righted, they show life only by immediately rolling upside down again.

Only two of the three species occur in Florida. These two are specialist feeders on toads.

Hog-nosed snakes have enlarged teeth in the rear of the upper jaw (but rarely bite, no matter how disturbed they become), and their saliva contains toxins. On the rare occasions when humans are bitten by these snakes, some have experienced lividity, tenderness, and quite considerable swelling at the bite site. Despite their tendency not to bite, wild hog-nosed snakes should be handled with care.

Hog-nosed snakes are egg-layers that tend to be active by day.

The hog-nosed snakes are stout for their length. They have a moderately to prominently upturned and dorsally keeled rostral scale, from 23 to 25 rows of keeled body scales, and a divided anal plate.

These are snakes of open sandy areas, including sparsely wooded and agri-cultural areas.

## 66. Eastern Hog-nosed Snake
### *Heterodon platirhinos*

**Nonvenomous** In the strictest sense of accu-racy, it should be stated that the eastern hog-nosed snake does produce a slightly toxic sa-liva but is not dangerously venomous to humans.

**Size** Most examples seen are between 18 and 30 inches in length. This species occasionally attains 3½ feet in length.

**Identification** A stocky snake, the hog-nosed snake is typified by a proportionately large head, a thick neck, and a short tail. The top of the head is dark in color. The scale on the tip of the nose is large, pointed, keeled dorsally, but *not* strongly upturned. This large scale gives the hog-nosed snakes the ability to root buried toads (found by scent) out of their sandy burrows. This interesting snake occurs in a multitude of colors. The ground colors most commonly seen are light to medium brown or sandy gray. However, ground colors of red, yellowish-tan, tan, grayish-green, and black are also known. The black specimens begin life as gray individuals with typical patterns. As they age, melanin suffuses the scales until the pattern is virtually overwhelmed and the entire snake is black. Examples with lighter ground colors are usually very strongly patterned, having a series of dark dorsal blotches as well as smaller alternating lateral blotches (some examples can be remarkably similar in appearance to dusky pygmy rattlesnakes). The belly is usually gray to almost black and is patterned with lighter spots. The underside of the tail is lighter than the belly color. When the snake is disturbed, its tail is often rather tightly coiled. The keeled scales are in 23 or 25 rows; the anal plate is divided.

**Behavior** When on the defensive, the eastern hog-nosed snake can put on a venomous snake look-alike act that can convince most casual watchers that it is at least dangerous, if not deadly. But the hissing, hood spreading, and striking that the snake routinely indulges in is all an act. In reality, the hog-nosed snake is one of our most innocuous serpents, despite the mildly venomous properties of its saliva.

Typical behavior patterns of this snake include hiding its head beneath the tightly coiled body and elevating the coiled tail to draw the attention of the predator; coiling and striking (usually with the mouth closed); flattening its neck (but *not* elevating its head) into an elongate hood; discharging musk and smearing feces; and feigning death.

The latter act usually comes only after the others fail to frighten a predator away. The act of feigning death is complex. The snake will appear to go into a series of convulsions, writhing from side to side. During these throes, regurgitation of food may occur. Finally the snake rolls upside down, mouth partially open, and becomes limp. It would be a perfect act were it not for one thing—if you roll the snake right-side up, it will roll upside down again. If left for a few minutes to its own devices, so that it thinks that it is safe, the snake will roll over and crawl slowly away.

**Habitat/Range** Where there are toads, there may be eastern hog-nosed snakes. This snake is most commonly seen in areas with moderately sandy soil (this covers most of Florida). Look for it in pinewoods and well-drained, open, mixed woodlands.

The eastern hog-nosed snake is found throughout mainland Florida, as well as across the eastern United States from southern New England to southeastern South Dakota and eastern Texas.

**Abundance** Until the mid-twentieth century, the eastern hog-nosed snake was a common snake in many areas of Florida. Although still found, it seems no longer common, even in areas of ideal habitat that continue to harbor sizable populations of toads.

**Prey** Despite the toxic secretions (bufotoxins) produced by toads, these amphibians are the primary prey of the eastern hog-nosed snake. Enlarged adrenal glands efficiently neutralize the bufotoxins ingested by the snake.

Besides the toxins, toads present a second problem. When frightened or grasped, they tend to inflate their body with air, becoming almost round in appearance. This is where the elongate rear teeth and the venomous saliva of the hog-nosed snakes come into play. The snake swallows the toad as far as possible and then employs the hinged, enlarged, fanglike rear teeth, which puncture the body of the toad and allow the entry of the toxic saliva. The toad soon becomes limp, deflates, and is easily swallowed. Occasionally, the elongated rear teeth of a large hog-nosed snake may actually puncture and mechanically deflate a struggling toad.

**Reproduction** Although the normal clutch of an eastern hog-nosed snake consists of 10 to 20 eggs, occasional clutches contain up to 40.

**Similar snakes** The southern hog-nosed snake has a much more prominently upturned rostral scale than the eastern, and the underside of the southern hog-nosed snake's tail is not strikingly different from the belly color. Black racers are slender and have a satiny luster to their scales. Indigo snakes have very shiny scales. Pygmy rattlesnakes have a tiny but easily discernible tail-tip rattle and facial pits. The southern copperhead has darker bands (not dorsal and lateral blotches) and a facial pit.

## 67. Southern Hog-nosed Snake
*Heterodon simus*

**Nonvenomous** Like its relatives, this snake produces a slightly toxic saliva but is not dangerously venomous to humans.

**Size** At a record length of only 24 inches, adults of this species are much smaller than those of the eastern hog-nosed snake. Typically, southern hog-nosed snakes are only 15 to 20 inches in length.

**Identification** The southern hog-nosed snake is of much more uniform ground color than the eastern species. The ground colors most commonly seen are light grayish-tan to sandy gray. Strongly delineated dorsal and alternating dorsolateral blotches are present. The belly coloration is light and may or may not be smudged with dark pigment. The underside of the tail is the same color as the belly. When the snake is disturbed, its tail is often rather tightly coiled. The scale on the tip of the nose (which is the scale that gives these snakes their hoglike rooting ability) is large, pointed, keeled dorsally, and distinctly upturned.

However, like the other species in this genus, the southern hog-nosed snakes have a proportionately large head, a thick neck, and a short tail. It is a stocky snake. The top of the southern hog-nosed snake's head is strongly patterned with black on gray or buff.

There are usually 25 rows of keeled scales; the anal plate is divided.

**Behavior** The habits and habitats of this small hog-nosed snake remain poorly understood. It will hiss, flatten its neck, and whip from side to side when frightened. The southern hog-nosed snake also will elevate and coil the tail to draw the attention of a predator and will discharge musk feces when lifted. This species is far less inclined to feign death than the larger eastern hog-nosed snake. Despite its bluff, the southern hog-nosed snake is not at all inclined to bite. They also seem less inclined to hide their head beneath their coils than do the eastern hog-nosed snakes.

**Habitat/Range** This small and distinctive hog-nosed snake is found in scattered colonies in areas of sandy substrate. They may be found in habitats as diverse as pinewoods or meadows, and coastal strand or turkey oak hammocks.

This species ranges southward and westward in the coastal plain from central eastern North Carolina to southern Mississippi. A disjunct colony is found in central Georgia. It occurs pretty much over the northern half of the Florida peninsula as well over as the entire panhandle. It is absent from many areas along Florida's eastern coast.

**Abundance** Rare in some areas but merely uncommon in others, the southern hog-nosed snake is not easily found in Florida. Nor does it seem to be particularly common outside of the Sunshine State.

**Prey** Like the eastern hog-nosed snake, the southern hog-nosed snake preys primarily on toads. The bufotoxins—the toxins manufactured by the toads—are neutralized by the snake's enlarged adrenal glands.

To overpower their toad prey (the toads inflate their body when grasped), southern hog-nosed snakes employ their long, rear, hinged, fanglike teeth. The snake's toxic saliva gains entrance through the tooth wounds. Soon following envenomation, the toad becomes limp, deflates, and is easily swallowed.

**Reproduction** A normal clutch for a southern hog-nosed snake consists of 4 to 9 eggs. Up to 14 in a clutch have been reported.

**Similar snakes** The eastern hog-nosed snake has a much less prominently upturned rostral scale than the southern, and the underside of the eastern hog-nosed snake's tail is lighter in color than the belly. Pygmy rattlesnakes have a tiny but easily discernible tail-tip rattle and facial pits.

# Introduced and Peripheral Nonvenomous Snakes

Florida has proven to be a paradise for numerous alien species of reptiles and amphibians. There are now about sixty species and subspecies found with regularity in the state. Of this number, six are snakes. Of these six, three are known to breed in Florida and have been established for a decade or more. The remaining three are popular pet-trade forms, and although they are not yet known to breed in the state, escapees or specimens deliberately released are found with amazing regularity.

## File Snakes, Family Acrochordidae

Except for two other species of file snakes, there is nothing quite like this snake in appearance. In appearance, these aquatic snakes somewhat resemble a knobby bicycle tire inner tube.

The members of this family occur in fresh, brackish, and saltwater habitats in the Australasian region.

These nonvenomous snakes feed upon fish, catching them with a quick sideways snap as the fish passes. If the fish is small, it is quickly swallowed. If the fish is large, it is held tightly in a body coil and manipulated for easier swallowing.

**Acrochordine husbandry** In Florida, this snake remains rare and localized, but imported specimens are occasionally seen in the pet trade. This snake is entirely aquatic and should be set up in a suitably sized, filtered aquarium. These snakes seem well adapted to low-light situations, so tank illumination is not needed. The pH of its water seems of little consequence to the snake's well-being, but to prevent the snake from developing serious skin lesions, the water must be ammonia- and bacteria-free. This rather amazing-appearing snake eats fish (and perhaps tadpoles) and prefers fair-sized minnows. A water temperature of 80 to 85°F seems fine.

## 68. Javan File (Elephant-trunk) Snake
### *Acrochordus javanicus*

**Nonvenomous** This snake has long teeth and could bite, but it almost never does. It is nonvenomous.

**Size** The Javan file snake attains an adult length of more than 6 feet. Males are the smaller sex.

**Identification** Its vernacular name of elephant-trunk snake rather accurately describes this species. File snake is also eminently accurate. When seen, the file snake imparts the impression of a size-6 snake in a size-8 skin. The dorsal color of this snake is olive-brown with poorly defined olive-green mottling, ocelli, or spots. The ventral coloration is lighter. There are no enlarged ventral scales. The scales are rough and filelike, ideal for penetrating the slime coating of a fish and securely restraining it in the snake's coils once caught. The eyes are small and directed dorsolaterally. The nostrils are high on the snout, close together, and directed forward. The tongue has very long forks that separate widely when protruded.

**Behavior** Awkward on land, this is a graceful snake in the water. It is fully aquatic and seems to be most active—or at least most frequently seen—at night. Then the snakes emerge from the fissures in the oolitic limestone bedrock of their pond and swim slowly through the beds of hydrilla and glasswort in search of fish. The most common fish in the few ponds in which this snake is found seems to be introduced *Tilapia,* large cichlids now used as food fish by humans. The nose of a file snake may occasionally be seen breaking the water surface. When illuminated by the beam of a flashlight, the snake quickly recoils and seeks subsurface refuge.

**Habitat/Range** This species is known to exist in a few manmade ponds in Dade County. Rumor has it that the snake's presence in Florida is the result of a deliberate introduction by a reptile dealer.

**Abundance** This is a rare and local species in Florida.

**Prey** It appears that this curious snake eats only fish.

**Reproduction** The reproductive biology of this snake in Florida is unknown. It is a live-bearing species that in Asia has clutches of more than 30 babies.

**Similar snakes** No Florida snake is even remotely similar to the file snake.

# Boas and Pythons, Family Boidae

The world's largest snakes are contained in this family. There are, however, also a great many diminutive species of boas and pythons. All are powerful constrictors that are capable of overpowering and consuming comparatively large prey animals. Boas and pythons have long been staples in the pet trade and are sold annually to hobbyists by the thousands. Hobbyists find them interesting and easily kept when babies, but few people are truly prepared for and capable of maintaining the giant species when they near adulthood. Those wishing to divest themselves of a large constricting snake soon find that the market is very limited.

Of the three species of boas and pythons we will mention, one—the Burmese python—has the potential for attaining or rarely exceeding 15 feet in length. The Colombian boa may reach 8 to 12 feet in length, and the ball python seldom exceeds 6 feet. Of these three, only the Colombian boa is known with certainty to be breeding in Florida, and it is the most localized and rarely seen of the trio. Burmese pythons in the 6 to 10-foot-long range and adult ball pythons are frequently found. Occasional examples of the potentially gigantic reticulated python (adult at up to 30 feet in length!) have been found in Florida, but they are rarely seen, and it has not so far been suggested that the species might be breeding here.

The pythons and boas are of interest, for they retain vestiges of hind limbs that are visible as a "spur" on each side of the vent. These are larger on males than on females and are used during the courtship procedures.

**Boid husbandry** These snakes are immensely popular with hobbyists, at least if they are of small species, or if of a large type, when the snakes are young and easy to handle. Understandably, the larger boas and pythons lose some of their allure when they attain a heavy-bodied 7 or 8 feet in length and become cumbersome to care for. At that length, some of the pythons are only about one-third grown. Most of the pythons now seen in Florida are either adult ball pythons (4 to 6 feet in length) or one-half- to one-third-grown Burmese pythons (8 to 12 feet in length). Although ball pythons do not typically bite, a large Burmese will typically challenge its captor. An 8-footer can be a serious adversary. If handling is misjudged, a python that size or larger can actually be a lethal antagonist. Always use great care when approaching large feral pythons.

Caging size must be geared to the size of the snake being kept. Because most of these snakes are slow and deliberate in their movements, they do not require overly large cages, but they do need enough space to move about. Unless handled frequently and gently, Burmese pythons may be difficult to handle. Although they do not require elevated perches or platforms, many of these snakes will use these if they are provided. These snakes will often bask and soak in a water receptacle if these are spacious enough. Although boas and Burmese pythons usually feed well on rodents and rabbits, ball pythons may take considerable teasing to induce a feeding response. Ball pythons have been known to refuse food for up to a year before deciding to eat.

These are all tropical snakes, and although a slight temperature gradient is desirable, a temperature between 84 and 90°F on the hot end of the cage will suffice.

## 69. Colombian (Common) Boa Constrictor
*Boa constrictor imperator*

**Nonvenomous** Although nonvenomous, the Colombian boa is often defensive when approached. A large example can deliver a serious bite. Wounds should be cleansed well and dressed.

**Size** Most adults seen are in the 5 to 7-foot range, but this snake has the potential of attaining 12 feet in length. Neonates are about 14½ inches in length.

**Identification** This is a beautiful and heavy-bodied snake, the pattern of which has been likened to that of an oriental tapestry. Colombian boas are predominantly tan to light brown in color anteriorly, crossed by wide, darker brown saddles that extend as triangles midway down the sides. The saddles widen and shade to a beautiful, variable (but often deep) red posteriorly. The red of the tail is separated by white crossbands. The top of the head is the same tan as the body, and it bears a darker central longitudinal bar from the snout to the anterior nape. There is a dark bar anterior to the eye extending from the canthus to the lip and a dark eye-stripe. The belly is lighter than the back and is peppered or spotted with darker pigment. Neonates are paler than the adults, but the colors are the brightest on juvenile to subadult boas. The belly plates are proportionately small.

**Behavior** Although these boas may be relatively mellow, some are exactly the opposite—coiling, hissing, and striking at the slightest provocation. This is a slow-moving snake that depends on ambush to secure its prey. Once secured, the prey is immobilized and then killed by the powerful coils. These snakes may be seen thermoregulating in sunny spots on cool mornings. They are most active in the early evening, but during truly hot weather they may remain active long after dark.

**Habitat/Range** In Florida, this snake is found only in Miami, where it has been breeding for fifteen or more years. It is most frequently seen in pine woodlands amidst jumbles of oolitic limestone boulders.

**Abundance** Although it is regularly seen, the range of the Colombian boa in Florida does not seem to have increased in the last two decades, nor—even in the area where it is well-established—is the snake seen in any great numbers. We consider it an uncommon species. The natural range of this snake is from Mexico to Colombia.

**Prey** Hatchlings are opportunistic feeders. They may eat either invertebrate or vertebrate prey. Adults prefer to eat mammals and birds. In Florida, it is probable that squirrels and opossums are the main dietary items of adult boas, but small raccoons and feral cats are probably also eaten.

**Reproduction** This is a live-bearing snake that, in its natural range, produces large clutches of relatively large neonates. Its reproductive biology in Florida is unknown.

**Similar snakes** The pattern of dorsal saddles and warm brown body that shades to maroon or red on the tail is distinctive. There are no similarly colored snakes in Florida.


## 70. Burmese Python
*Python molurus bivittatus*

**Nonvenomous** Although nonvenomous, a large Burmese python is often very ready to bite and can be a dangerous adversary. We urge that if you are alone, you do not approach a specimen more than 8 feet long. A large example can deliver a serious bite, and the constricting coils can be life-threatening. Bite wounds should be cleansed well and dressed.

**Size** This is the largest snake species regularly found in Florida. Most adults seen are in the 7 to 12-foot range, but this snake has the potential of exceeding 20 feet in length. Hatchlings are about 14 to 18 inches in length.

**Identification** The Burmese python is a study in browns, tans, and black. Despite its dark color, it is a very attractive snake. When it is healthy, a pretty iridescence will be seen to play over the scales of this heavy-bodied snake. The ground color is tan, but the black-edged brown pattern is difficult to describe. There is a pattern of irregular dark dorsal saddles. Lateral blotches of irregular shape are also present, and these are often dark-edged posteriorly. The comparatively narrow belly scales are light tan. The top of the head is adorned with a dark spearpoint, with the sharp end at the tip of the snout. There is a dark eye-stripe. Neonates are colored and patterned like the adults.

**Behavior** Quite tractable when regularly handled, an escaped python soon takes on the mien of a wild snake. Most large examples approached in the wild will coil, hiss, and strike. This is a slow-moving snake that depends on ambush to secure its prey. Once secured, the prey is immobilized and then killed by the powerful coils. Little is known about these snakes in Florida. Most found have been active during the day, but a few large specimens seen in Everglades National Park were active well after nightfall.

**Habitat/Range** This snake is most commonly found prowling on summer days in city lots or parks, indicating that they are relatively recent escapees or releases. Burmese pythons are regularly found from Pensacola to Jacksonville and south to Florida's Everglades. How far north on the peninsula a Burmese python can over-winter is not yet known.

**Abundance** Although it is regularly seen, we still consider the Burmese python an uncommon species in Florida. The natural range of this snake is Southeast Asia, Malaysia, and Indonesia.

**Prey** Both hatchlings and adults feed opportunistically on mammals and small birds. In Florida, it is probable that mice and small rats are the prey of juvenile Burmese pythons, and that squirrels and opossums are main dietary items of the adult pythons. Small raccoons and feral cats are probably also eaten.

**Reproduction** The reproductive biology of the Burmese python is known in Florida only from captive specimens. This is an oviparous snake that, in its natural range and in captivity, produces large clutches of large eggs. Although a clutch normally numbers between 20 and 40 eggs, more than 60 have been recorded. The female Burmese python coils around and incubates her eggs.

**Similar snakes** Pattern, color, and size should identify this snake. See also the account for the ball python.

**Comment** Burmese pythons are not yet known to breed in Florida. Those found are likely either escapees or illegally released individuals. This is another of the snakes in which herpetoculturists have developed numerous designer colors and patterns. It is entirely feasible that Burmese pythons of aberrant colors are also loose in Florida. Use extreme care when approaching a large python. It is illegal to release a non-native snake in Florida.

## 71. Ball Python
### *Python regius*

**Nonvenomous** This small and innocuous python is being found with increasing frequency in Florida. They seldom bite, but should they happen to, the wounds should be cleansed well and dressed.

**Size** This is a small but very heavy-bodied snake. Ball pythons are adult at about 5 (rarely to 6) feet in length. Hatchlings are about 10 inches in length.

**Identification** Like the Burmese python, the much smaller ball python is clad in scales of tan, brown, and black. However, unlike the Burmese python—which has a very regular dorsal pattern of blotches—the ball python has an irregular dorsal pattern but a regular pattern of large, *rounded,* light lateral markings. Each light lateral blotch contains a small dark oval. The top of the ball python's head is dark. The belly scales are narrow and are light tan. There is a dark eye-stripe. Neonates are colored and patterned like the adults.

**Behavior** This is a pretty and innocuous snake. Although it may hiss when approached, if startled or handled this python usually rolls itself into a ball with its head protected by the coils. This slow-moving snake is a wait-and-ambush hunter. Once secured, the prey is immobilized and then killed by the powerful coils. Little is known about these snakes in Florida. Most found have been active during the day.

**Comment** It is thought that the many ball pythons being found in Florida are accidental escapees or are deliberately released. Ball pythons are not yet known to breed in Florida. It is illegal to release a non-native snake in Florida.

**Habitat/Range** This snake is most commonly found prowling on summer days in residential areas, indicating that they are relatively recent escapees or releases. These snakes are being found in cities throughout the state. Whether these little pythons will eventually breed in Florida, or whether they can even survive one of the state's colder winters, is not yet known.

**Abundance** Although it is regularly seen, we still consider the ball python an uncommon species in Florida. The natural range of this snake is tropical West Africa.

**Prey** The preferred prey of the ball python in Florida is unknown.

**Reproduction** This snake is an oviparous species that produces a small clutch (usually 5 to 8) of large eggs once annually. It is not thought that the ball python is yet reproducing in Florida.

**Similar snakes** This snake is apt to be confused with a small Burmese python. Please check the account for the latter on page 134. Burmese pythons usually have triangular or rhomboidal lateral spots with dark posterior edging. The light lateral spots of a ball python are more rounded and are bordered on all sides by black pigment. Also, the top of a ball python's head is dark and does not bear a spearpoint marking.


## Typical Snakes, Family Colubridae


## Kingsnakes, Bullsnakes, and Rat Snakes, Subfamily Lampropeltinae

For comments on this family and subfamily, please see page 52.

### 72. California Kingsnake
*Lampropeltis getula californiae*

**Nonvenomous** Like all other kingsnakes, this subspecies is devoid of venom. It is usually of relatively placid disposition and is considered an easily handled snake. Should you happen to be bitten, cleanse and dress the wound.

**Size** Although 3 to 3½ feet in length is the normal size of this snake, some California kingsnakes may near 5 feet in length. Hatchlings are about 8 to 11 inches in length.

**Identification** The ground color of the normal phase of the California kingsnake is black or very deep brown, and the snake has pattern of broad white crossbands. The nose and face are largely white. A second phase (see "comments" section below) is devoid of crossbands but has a stark white vertebral stripe. The stripe may be entire or broken one or more times along its length. Again, the face is largely white. The smooth dorsal scales are in 23 or 25 rows, and the anal plate is undivided.

**Behavior** In its natural habitat and range (the Pacific coast of the United States and Baja California), this is a secretive snake. It is active by day during cool weather but becomes largely nocturnal during the hot days and nights of summer. No particular activity pattern has yet been noted for specimens found in Florida.

**Habitat/Range** It is not yet known whether the California kingsnake can survive for extended periods in Florida, but it probably can. Those found have been in residential areas, many of them in large cities such as Miami and Tampa. Most found have been surface-active rather than hiding (as our native kingsnake populations are wont to do) beneath surface debris (such as boards and cardboard, roofing tins).

**Abundance** In Florida, this is still an uncommon subspecies. It is thought that the populations of California kingsnakes in the Sunshine State are currently sustained and replenished by escaped or released individuals rather than by offspring from established feral breeding groups.

**Prey** Kingsnakes in general have a remarkably varied diet. Both ectothermic (cold-blooded) and endothermic (warm-blooded) prey are accepted.

**Reproduction** A normal clutch contains from 3 to 10 eggs. This race of kingsnake is not yet known to breed in Florida.

**Similar snakes** With their shiny scales, rounded nose, and distinct markings, this kingsnake would not be easily confused with any other snake in Florida.

**Comments** Like corn snakes, herpetoculturists now breed California kingsnakes in ten or more color phases and patterns. Albinos; specimens with the white stripes that occupy more than half of the scale rows; those with a lavender ground color; many with both stripes and bands—these are all now commonly seen color phases. The California kingsnake is not yet known to breed in Florida, but escaped or released specimens are frequently found, primarily in residential areas. It is possible that this snake could interbreed with our native kingsnakes of this complex.

## Typical Blind Snakes, Family Typhlopidae

The three genera in this primarily tropical family contain more than 160 species. All are persistent burrowers. None is native to the United States, but one—the Asian Brahminy blind snake—has been introduced to the southern half of peninsular Florida and has now been found elsewhere in Florida and in the Lower Rio Grande Valley of Texas as well. In this family, the maxillary bones are toothed and are *not* fused solidly to the skull. The lower jawbones bear no teeth.

### 73. Brahminy Blind (Flowerpot) Snake
*Ramphotyphlops braminus*

**Nonvenomous** This—the smallest snake species of Florida—is completely devoid of venom and far too small to bite any hand that holds it.
**Size** This minuscule snake is adult at from 3 to 5 inches in length. It is also proportionately slender, a large adult being about the diameter of a knitting needle.
**Identification** Normally a shiny black above and below, when this little snake prepares to shed its

skin it becomes an opalescent purple in color. There are no enlarged belly scales and no visible eyes. The tail—which is tipped by a spinelike scale—is nearly as blunt as the head. The scales are in 14 rows, but it will take a hand lens to ascertain this. There is no enlarged anal plate. The Brahminy blind snake is so divergent from the popular concept of a snake that many folks who see it think it to be a strange worm.
**Behavior** One word describes the behavior of the tiny snake—*burrowing*. Because of one of its favored habitats, the tiny Brahminy blind snake is often referred to as the flowerpot snake.

**Habitat/Range** This introduced tropical Asian snake is now common on the southern one-fourth of the Florida peninsula and has been found in Highlands, Palm Beach, Pinellas, Santa Rosa, and Duval Counties as well. It may be incapable of surviving winters north of the Tampa–St. Petersburg region, but populations are continually replenished when potted plants are brought north from South Florida nurseries.

**Abundance** In South Florida, this is now an abundant snake. The Pinellas County population also seems to be growing.

**Prey** This fossorial snake feeds largely on ant and termite pupae. It is probable that the eggs and pupae of other tiny burrowing insects are also eaten.

**Reproduction** The Brahminy blind snake is a unisexual, all-female, parthenogenetic, oviparous species.

**Similar snakes** None.

# Peripheral Nonvenomous Snakes

The ranges of several harmless, and one venomous, snake species come virtually to the Florida state line. There is no reason to believe that eventually one or more of these kinds will not be found in Florida. One, the worm snake, is known from fossil records to occur in Florida. We have included an account for the worm snake below and have made cursory mention of other peripherals.

## Typical Snakes, Family Colubridae

## Kingsnakes, Bullsnakes, and Rat Snakes, Subfamily Lampropeltinae

### 74. Speckled Kingsnake
### *Lampropeltis getula holbrooki*

The pretty and aptly named speckled kingsnake is adult at 3 to 5½ feet in length. Each black dorsal and lateral scale usually bears a yellow dot of variable intensity. In addition, the chain pattern so typical of the eastern kingsnakes is usually at least weakly visible. The specimens that abut the Florida state line are considered intergrades between the speckled and eastern kingsnakes. This snake inhabits open woodlands; woodland clearings and edges; meadows and their edges; ditch, canal, and pond edges; and the edges of swamps, marshes, and impoundments. The edges of dumps and trash piles are especially favored sites, as are the sunny, grassy slopes of embankments and dikes.

## 75. Black Pine Snake
### *Pituophis melanoleucus lodingi*

This snake is a 5 to 6-foot-long burrowing inhabitant of first- and second-growth longleaf pine forests. It ranges westward from the westernmost tip of the Florida panhandle through southeastern Mississippi, and Washington Parish, Louisiana. By far the darkest of the pine snakes, adults are so dark that it is often difficult to define a pattern. The snake may be entirely black, or black anteriorly and vaguely patterned with gray posteriorly. The venter is dark but often somewhat lighter than the dorsum.

# Water Snakes and Garter Snakes, Family Colubridae

## Water Snakes, Subfamily Natricinae

## 76. Broad-banded x Banded Water Snake
### *Nerodia fasciata confluens* x *N. f. fasciata*

The broad-banded water snake x banded water snake intergrade is known scientifically as *Nerodia fasciata confluens* x *N. f. fasciata.*

This snake is adult at between 24 and 40 inches. The record size is 45 inches. It occurs from southeastern Louisiana right up to the Alabama-Florida state line on Florida's western panhandle. Both the ground color and pattern of this intergrade water snake are variable. The ground color may be gray, tan, olive, or almost black. The pattern may be dark-olive, greenish-brown, old rose, or red. The bands are often the darkest at their outer edges. There are not usually any dark lateral spots between the dark bands, but there may be light areas in the dark bands. Some of these water snakes are so dark that they may appear almost unicolored. The belly is off-white to white and has an irregular pattern of darker (sometimes a quite bright red) pigment. The upper labial scales are usually outlined by dark pigment. A dark stripe may run from the back of the eye to the rear of the angle of the jaw.

## Colubrid Snakes with Unresolved Affinities

### Worm Snakes, Genus *Carphophis*

Depending on the views of a researcher, this genus may contain either one species with three subspecies or two full species, the easternmost with two subspecies. The latter view is now rather generally accepted.

These are small burrowing snakes with smooth, shiny scales arranged in 13 rows. Except when colors are muted by approaching ecdysis (shedding), a beautiful opalescent sheen plays over the scales. The head is small and pointed; the eyes are small. The tail terminates in a sharpened, spiny tip. The anal plate is divided.

### 77. Midwest Worm Snake
#### *Carphophis amoenus helenae*

**Nonvenomous** This is a harmless and entirely in-nocuous species that ordinarily cannot be made to bite.
**Size** A tiny burrowing snake, the Midwest worm snake is adult at from 8 to 11 inches.
**Identification** This pretty, shiny-scaled snake is warm brown above and opalescent pink below. Besides the belly scales, the lowest one or two rows of lateral scales are pink. The tail tip ends in a

spinelike scale. The eyes are very small but very obvious. There is a reduction of scale numbers (from the arrangement of most snakes) on the snout, for each prefrontal is fused with the corresponding internasal scale.
**Behavior** Worthy of reiteration are the facts that the worm snake neither bites nor is prone to smearing cloacal contents on a captor. If held, the little snake merely tries to escape by pushing between fingers with its nose or with the

sharply pointed tail. This snake burrows extensively and is seldom surface-active.

**Habitat/Range** Open woodlands, rock-strewn hillsides and fields, trash dumps, and similar habitats are the habitats of this burrowing snake. It ranges southward from central Ohio and Illinois to western Georgia and eastern Louisiana. In Alabama, it has been found virtually to the Florida state line along Florida's western panhandle.

**Abundance** This is a common to abundant snake, but because of its secretive habits, it is very easily overlooked.

**Prey** Earthworms are the preferred prey, but soft-bodied insect larvae are reportedly also consumed.

**Reproduction** Clutches of 1 to 6, more rarely to 8, thin-shelled eggs are laid in or beneath moisture-retaining logs and debris. The incubation lasts between 7 and 9 weeks. Hatchlings average 3½ inches in length.

**Similar snakes** Throughout most of its range, this is the only small snake with 13 rows of smooth scales and on which the belly color extends upward to the lowermost row or two of lateral scales.

## Ring-necked Snakes

### 78. Mississippi Ring-necked Snake
*Diadophis punctatus stictogenys*

Although the Mississippi ring-necked snake is not actually considered a component of Florida's herpetofauna, examples bearing the identification characteristics of this race are occasionally found from the Apalachicola River westward. Most specimens seen are between 10 and 14 inches in length, but occasional examples may near 18 inches in length. This little woodland snake has a dorsal ground color of slate-gray,  blue-gray, or olive. A satiny luster of the smooth dorsal and lateral scales imparts a look of sleekness to this and other ring-necked snakes. The neck-ring of the Mississippi ring-necked snake is usually broken vertebrally. The ring may be yellow to orange. The yellow-orange to orange belly usually bears a double row of small black dots. The subcaudal scales are usually brighter orange than those of the belly. Where intergradation with the southern ring-necked snake occurs in eastern Alabama and on the western Florida panhandle, the belly spotting may be more irregular. Hatchlings are darker than the adults and have a paler collar. This is primarily a woodland snake, but it often hides beneath surface debris in more open areas.

# Florida habitats

A. Evening, especially with a thunderstorm brewing and barometric pressure lowering, is a preferred period for surface activity for snakes.

B. Woodland habitats are often rejuvenated by fire.

C. Oaks of several species, rosemary, and saw palmetto are characteristic xeric habitats for pine snakes, coachwhips, crowned snakes, and diamond-backed rattle-snakes.

D. On the Florida Keys, scrubland with fragmented oolitic limestone ground cover is the habitat of the very rare rim rock crowned snake, the eastern coral snake, and the Key ring-necked snake.

F. Palm and mixed hardwood hammocks of South Florida provide habitat for yellow rat snakes, corn snakes, and coral snakes.

E. Diamond-backed rattlesnakes, Florida worm lizards, crowned snakes, black racers, and indigo snakes are at home on the rapidly drained sandhills of interior Central Florida.

G. Yellow rat snakes and occasionally rough green snakes may seek seclusion in arboreal bromeliads.

H. Naturally occurring woodland clearings are ideal areas to find black racers and ring-necked snakes.

I. Pine-palmetto scrublands are good habitats for diamond-backed rattlesnakes, pine woods snakes, garter snakes, racers, and an occasional kingsnake.

J. Pine-oak woodlands in North Florida harbor gray rat snakes, racers, and scarlet kingsnakes.

K. Yellow rat snakes and corn snakes may be found resting in the broken boots of sabal palms.

L. Flooded hard-woods may provide ideal habitats for some water snakes, crayfish snakes, and mud snakes.

M. Look for rat snakes and rough green snakes in cypress stands; their related ponds are ideal for water snakes, crayfish snakes, swamp snakes, and cottonmouths.

N. Hydric prairies, seasonally carpeted with wildflowers, are excellent habitats for racers, kingsnakes, garter snakes, pygmy rattlesnakes, and cottonmouths.

O. Human-generated debris, sometimes amazingly close to habitations still in use, provide excellent microhabitats for many snake species.

P. The rafter systems of accessible but unused outbuildings are favored by all of the rat snakes.

Q. Salt marshes are home to salt marsh snakes, a specialized species of water snake.

R. Mangrove salt marsh snakes utilize stands of their namesake tree as habitats throughout much of their range.

*Above:* S. The spring runs in Florida's interior are home to many species of water snakes, ribbon snakes, and rainbow snakes.

*Left:* T. Unkempt canal edges can harbor snakes of many species, including the venomous cottonmouths, as well as many snake predators such as this American bittern.

U. Along the small streams in Florida's panhandle, southern copperheads and small woodland burrowing snakes occur.

V. Stumps protruding from quiet waters offer basking sites to many natricine and other water-oriented snakes.

W. The root systems of floating vegetation are favored by crayfish snakes.

X. The shores and shallows of ephemeral ponds provide a wonderful array of temporary habitats for kingsnakes, garter snakes, and many others.

# Miscellaneous subjects

Y. Many snakes assume a characteristic striking pose when frightened.

Z. Shed snake skins may be more easily seen than the snakes themselves.

AA. Many snakes produce eggs that are dependent on external climatic conditions to successfully incubate. Here, a hatching rough green snake makes its debut.

BB. Aptly named, a yellow rat snake consumes a rodent. Note the rows of recurved teeth in the snake's upper jaw.

# Other Legless Floridians

CC. Eastern slender glass lizard, *Ophisaurus attenuatus longicaudus*

DD. Island glass lizard, *Ophisaurus compressus*

EE. Mimic glass lizard, *Ophisaurus mimicus*

FF. Eastern glass
lizard, *Ophisaurus
ventralis*, normal
coloration

GG. Eastern glass
lizard, *Ophisaurus
ventralis*, old male

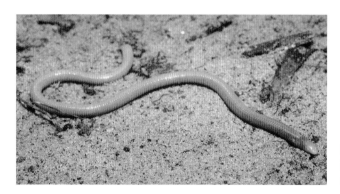

HH. Florida worm
lizard, *Rhineura
floridana*

II. Florida worm lizard,
*Rhineura floridana;* note
the shovel-like scale on tip
of snout.

# Florida's Snakes

1. Brown-chinned racer, *Coluber constrictor helvigularis*

2. Everglades racer, *Coluber constrictor paludicola*

3A. Southern black racer, *Coluber constrictor priapus*, adult

3B. Southern black racer, *Coluber constrictor priapus*, hatchling

4A. Eastern indigo snake, *Drymarchon corais couperi*

4B. Eastern indigo snake, *Drymarchon corais couperi*, head detail

5A. Eastern coachwhip, *Masticophis flagellum flagellum*, adult

5B. Eastern coachwhip, *Masticophis flagellum flagellum*, hatchling

6. Rough green snake, *Opheodrys aestivus*

7. Southeastern crowned snake, *Tantilla coronata*

8. Rim rock crowned snake, *Tantilla oolitica*

9. Central Florida crowned snake, *Tantilla relicta neilli*

10. Coastal dunes crowned snake, *Tantilla relicta pamlica*

11. Peninsula crowned snake, *Tantilla relicta relicta*

12A. Pine woods snake, *Rhadinea flavilata*

12B. Pine woods snake, *Rhadinea flavilata*, head detail showing light upper lips

13A. Florida scarlet snake, *Cemophora coccinea coccinea*, normal pattern

13B. Florida scarlet snake, *Cemophora coccinea coccinea*, aberrant pattern

14. Northern scarlet snake, *Cemophora coccinea copei;* note the immaculate belly.

15A. Corn snake, *Pantherophis (Elaphe) guttata guttata,* normal color

15B. Corn snake, *Pantherophis (Elaphe) guttata guttata,* anerythristic (melanistic) morph

15C. Corn snake, *Pantherophis* (*Elaphe*) *guttata guttata,* South Florida or Miami morph

15D. Corn snake, *Pantherophis* (*Elaphe*) *guttata guttata,* north-eastern Florida morph

16A. Corn snake, *Pantherophis* (*Elaphe*) *guttata guttata,* Lower Keys variant, rosy morph

16B. Corn snake, *Pantherophis (Elaphe) guttata guttata*, Lower Keys variant, silver morph

16C. Corn snake, *Pantherophis (Elaphe) guttata guttata*, Lower Keys variant, olive morph

17A. Yellow rat snake, *Pantherophis (Elaphe) obsoleta quadrivittata*, North Florida morph

17B. Yellow rat snake, *Pantherophis (Elaphe) obsoleta quadrivittata,* South Florida morph

18A. Yellow rat snake, *Pantherophis (Elaphe) obsoleta quadrivittata,* Upper Keys variant, aberrant color morph

18B. Yellow rat snake, *Pantherophis (Elaphe) obsoleta quadrivittata,* Upper Keys variant, normal morph

19. Everglades rat snake, *Pantherophis (Elaphe) obsoleta rossalleni*

20A. Gray rat snake, *Pantherophis (Elaphe) obsoleta spiloides*

20B. Hatchlings of the gray rat snake (*top*); yellow rat snake (*left*); and Everglades rat snake (*bottom*)

21. Gulf Hammock rat snake, *Pantherophis (Elaphe) obsoleta quadrivittata* x *P. (E.) o. spiloides*

22A. South Florida mole kingsnake, *Lampropeltis calligaster occipitolineata*

22B. South Florida mole kingsnake, *Lampropeltis calligaster occipitolineata*, detail of head

23A. Mole king-snake, *Lampro-peltis calligaster rhombomaculata*, gray morph

23B. Mole king-snake, *Lampro-peltis calligaster rhombomaculata*, gray morph, detail of head

23C. Mole king-snake, *Lampro-peltis calligaster rhombomaculata*, red morph

24A. Florida kingsnake, *Lampropeltis getula floridana,* adult

24B. Florida kingsnake, *Lampropeltis getula floridana,* hatchling

25. Eastern kingsnake, *Lampropeltis getula floridana*

26. Peninsula kingsnake, *Lampropeltis getula getula* x *L. g. floridana*

27A. Apalachi-cola lowland kingsnake, *Lampropeltis getula* ssp., dark-blotched variant

27B. Apalachi-cola lowland kingsnake, *Lampropeltis getula* ssp., light-blotched variant

27C. Apalachicola lowland kingsnake, *Lampropeltis getula* ssp., full-striped variant

27D. Apalachicola lowland kingsnake, *Lampropeltis getula* ssp., broken-striped variant

28A. Scarlet kingsnake, *Lampropeltis triangulum elapsoides*

28B. Scarlet kingsnake, *Lampropeltis triangulum elapsoides,* detail of head

29A. Florida pine snake, *Pituophis melanoleucus mugitus*

29B. Florida pine snake, *Pituophis melanoleucus mugitus,* detail of head; note the enlarged rostral (nose-tip) scale.

30. Florida x black pine snake, *Pituophis melanoleucus mugitus* x *P. m. lodingi,* naturally occurring intergrade

31A. Short-tailed snake, *Stilosoma extenuatum,* gray morph

31B. Short-tailed snake, *Stilosoma extenuatum,* red-backed morph

32A. Gulf salt marsh snake, *Nerodia clarkii clarkii*

32B. Gulf salt marsh snake x mangrove salt marsh snake, *Nerodia clarkii clarkii* x *N. c. compressicauda*, naturally occurring intergrade

33A. Mangrove salt marsh snake, *Nerodia clarkii compressicauda*, red morph

33B. Mangrove salt marsh snake, *Nerodia clarkii compressicauda,* dark morph

34. Atlantic salt marsh snake, *Nerodia clarkii taeniata* (photo by R. W. Van Devender)

35A. Mississippi green water snake, *Nerodia cyclopion;* note the strongly patterned belly.

35B. Mississippi green water snake, *Nerodia cyclopion*, detail of head

36A. Red-bellied water snake, *Nerodia erythrogaster erythrogaster*, adult

36B. Red-bellied water snake, *Nerodia erythrogaster erythrogaster*, neonate

37. Yellow-bellied water snake, *Nerodia erythrogaster flavigaster*

38. Banded water snake, *Nerodia fasciata fasciata*

39A. Florida water snake, *Nerodia fasciata pictiventris*, adult

39B. Florida water snake, *Nerodia fasciata pictiventris,* neonate

40A. Florida green water snake, *Nerodia floridana,* green morph

40B. Florida green water snake, *Nerodia floridana,* green morph; note the unpatterned belly.

40C. Florida green water snake, *Nerodia floridana,* South Florida red morph

41A. Midland water snake, *Nerodia sipedon pleuralis*

41B. Midland water snake, *Nerodia sipedon pleuralis,* detail of head

42A. Brown water snake, *Nerodia taxispilota*, normal and pallid (hypomelanistic?) examples

42B. Brown water snake, *Nerodia taxispilota*, normal morph; note complex belly pattern.

43. Striped crayfish snake, *Regina alleni*

44. Glossy crayfish snake, *Regina rigida rigida*

45. Gulf crayfish snake, *Regina rigida sinicola*

46. Queen snake, *Regina septemvittata*

47. South Florida swamp snake, *Seminatrix pygaea cyclas*

48. North Florida swamp snake, *Seminatrix pygaea pygaea*

49. Marsh brown snake, *Storeria dekayi limnetes*

50. Midland
brown snake,
*Storeria dekayi
wrightorum*

51. Florida red-
bellied snake,
*Storeria
occipitomaculata
obscura*

52A. Florida
brown snake,
*Storeria victa*,
tan morph

52B. Florida brown snake, *Storeria victa*, red morph

53. Blue-striped ribbon snake, *Thamnophis sauritus nitae*

54A. Peninsula ribbon snake, *Thamnophis sauritus sackenii*

54B. Peninsula ribbon snake, *Thamnophis sauritus sackenii,* detail of head; note the light vertical bar anterior to eye. This marking separates eastern ribbon snakes from garter snakes.

55. Eastern ribbon snake, *Thamnophis sauritus sauritus*

56. Blue-striped garter snake, *Thamnophis sirtalis similis*

57A. Eastern garter snake, *Thamnophis sirtalis sirtalis,* striped morph

57B. Eastern garter snake, *Thamnophis sirtalis sirtalis,* checkered morph

58A. Rough earth snake, *Virginia striatula,* gray morph

58B. Rough earth snake, *Virginia striatula*, brown morph

59. Eastern smooth earth snake, *Virginia valeriae valeriae*

60. Key ring-necked snake, *Diadophis punctatus acricus;* note the poorly defined neck-ring.

61. Southern ring-necked snake, *Diadophis punctatus punctatus;* note the very prominent belly spots.

62A. Eastern mud snake, *Farancia abacura abacura,* normal color and pattern

62B. Eastern mud snake, *Farancia abacura abacura,* abnormally intensified color

63. Western mud snake, *Farancia abacura reinwardtii*

64A. Common rainbow snake, *Farancia erytogramma erytogramma*, adult

64B. Common rainbow snake, *Farancia erytogramma erytogramma*, hatchling

65. South Florida rainbow snake, *Farancia erytogramma seminola,* preserved specimen

66A. Eastern hog-nosed snake, *Heterodon platirhinos,* normal blotched pattern

66B. Eastern hog-nosed snake, *Heterodon platirhinos,* black morph

67A. Southern hog-nosed snake, *Heterodon simus*

67B. Southern hog-nosed snake, *Heterodon simus,* detail of head; note the very prominently upturned rostral (nose-tip) scale.

68. Javan file snake, *Acrochordus javanicus*

69. Colombian boa constrictor, *Boa constrictor imperator*

70. Burmese python, *Python molurus bivittatus*

71A. Ball python, *Python regius*

71B. Ball python, *Python regius,* detail of head; note the heat receptor pits in labial (lip) scales.

72A. California kingsnake, *Lampropeltis getula californiae,* banded morph

72B. California kingsnake, *Lampropeltis getula californiae,* striped morph

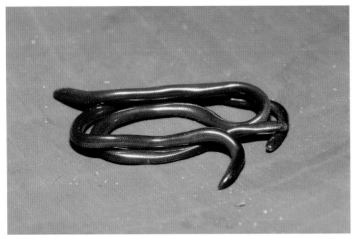

73. Brahminy blind snake, *Ramphotyphlops braminus*

74. Speckled kingsnake, *Lampropeltis getula holbrooki*

75. Black pine snake, *Pituophis melanoleucus lodingi*

76. Broad-banded x banded water snake, *Nerodia fasciata confluens* x *N. f. fasciata*

77. Midwest worm snake, *Carphophis amoena helenae*

78. Mississippi ring-necked snake, *Diadophis punctatus stictogenys;* note the tiny belly spots.

79A. Eastern coral snake, *Micrurus fulvius*, normal pattern

79B. Eastern coral snake, *Micrurus fulvius*, Upper Keys variant (photo by James Duquesnel)

80. Southern copperhead, *Agkistrodon contortrix contortrix*

81A. Florida cottonmouth, *Agkistrodon piscivorous conanti*, adult

81B. Florida cottonmouth, *Agkistrodon piscivorous conanti*, neonate

81C. Florida cottonmouth, *Agkistrodon piscivorous conanti*; note that the pattern is better defined when the snake is wet.

82. Eastern cottonmouth x Florida cottonmouth, *Agkistrodon piscivorous piscivorous* x *A. p. conanti,* adult defensively gaping

83A. Eastern diamond-backed rattlesnake, *Crotalus adamanteus*

83B. Eastern diamond-backed rattlesnake, *Crotalus adamanteus,* detail of head; note the heat sensory pits.

84A. Timber rattlesnake, *Crotalus horridus (atricaudatus)*, dark southeastern canebrake morph

84B. Timber rattlesnake, *Crotalus horridus (atricaudatus)*, light southeastern canebrake morph

84C. Timber rattlesnake x eastern diamond-backed rattlesnake, *Crotalus horridus (atricaudatus)* x *C. adamanteus*, rare naturally occurring hybrid

85A. Dusky pygmy rattle-snake, *Sistrurus miliarius barbouri*

85B. Dusky pygmy rattle-snake, *Sistrurus miliarius barbouri,* detail of head; note the lance shape.

86. Western cottonmouth, *Agkistrodon piscivorous leucostoma*

# VENOMOUS Snakes

# Native Snakes

## Elapid Snakes; Cobras and Allies, Family Elapidae

This family contains the coral snakes as well as the cobras, mambas, kraits, and their allies. Most are of Old World distribution, but three genera of coral snakes occur in the Americas. There are only two representatives in the eastern United States: the eastern coral snake (the proposed new common name is "harlequin coral snake") and the Texas coral snake. A small coral snake of a second genus is found in our southwestern states. The coral snakes of the United States are usually clad in rings of red, yellow, and black. The coral snakes of the Florida Keys can be very confusingly colored, often lacking most of the yellow (please note that this comment pertains only to coral snakes of the Keys!).

Coral snakes are common but secretive. They occur in habitats as diverse as isolated woodlands and suburban backyards and are surface-active during hot, wet weather. Despite being clad in colors that seem gaudy, these snakes are easily overlooked and blend well with their backgrounds.

Coral snakes have short, fixed (immovable) fangs, are dangerously venomous, and should not be handled. Any bite by a coral snake should have medical attention. The venom is predominantly neurotoxic. Thus, even a relatively painless bite can still be fatal.

**Elapine husbandry** State permits are required to keep any venomous snake in Florida. The coral snake is a pretty but nervous and demanding captive. These snakes require special handling; a securely locked cage (see state regulations) with several inches of burrowing substrate; a piece of bark beneath which to hide; a water dish; and a diet of snakes and lizards (of the latter, usually only skinks or glass lizards are accepted). A substrate having a thermal gradient (75–80°F cool end to 83–88°F hot end) should be provided. This will allow the snake to choose the temperature at which it is most comfortable at any given time.

Even when all of these criteria are met, coral snakes cannot be considered hardy captives. These are dangerously venomous snakes that are best not molested when found.


## Coral Snakes, Genus *Micrurus*

Only a single species of this genus (and family)—the eastern coral snake—is found in the eastern United States. The bright candy colors are legend, and these colors are shared by *nonvenomous* coral snake look-alikes. The *arrangement*—rather than the selection—of the colors is usually definitive. Throughout most of their range, the coral snakes of the United States have the two warning colors of a traffic signal (red and yellow) touching. This color pattern does not always hold true in Latin America and may not hold true on the Florida Keys. The nonvenomous coral snake look-alikes have the two warning colors separated by a ring of black.

There is a popular fallacy that because it has a small mouth, a coral snake must bite a finger, toe, or such to accomplish envenomation. It is also popularly thought that a coral snake must chew to administer its venom. Holding to these two beliefs could prove fatal, for neither could be further from the truth.

It is true that because of their short, rigid fangs, coral snakes are not capable of making the lunging strikes of the pit vipers. However, coral snakes are perfectly capable of biting an arm, leg, or foot. A single hurried bite by the snake is all that is necessary to accomplish envenomation. A third erroneous belief is that without preamble you can lift a coral snake safely by its tail. Coral snakes are nervous serpents that often react spastically to even a gentle touch. They can whip around, changing ends with amazing rapidity. If lifted by its tail, a coral snake may whip from side to side biting anything against which it bumps its head. *And* they can climb their own dangling body with disconcerting agility. *These are not snakes to be trifled with. Do not handle them!*

This snake utilizes habitats from suburban yards to open woodlands.

## 79. Eastern Coral Snake
### *Micrurus fulvius*

**Dangerously Venomous** Do not handle! This snake is far more agile than legends relate. Although they are not capable of making a lunging strike (like a rattlesnake), coral snakes can and will bite if molested.

**Size** The only elapine snake of Florida, the eastern coral snake has attained a record size of 4 feet. Those most commonly seen are between 20 and 36 inches in length. Hatchlings are about 7 inches long.

**Identification** The eastern coral snake has a somewhat flattened, relatively broad head. Its nose is usually black. The *normal* sequence of ring colors on the head and neck begins with black on the snout then continues yellow-black-yellow (note there is no red on the head or neck!). Similarly, the tail lacks red, being ringed only in black and yellow. The rings on the body are sequenced red-yellow-black-yellow-red—with the two caution colors touching. Many coral snakes have an encroachment of black pigment on the red scales.

Remember, *color aberrancies are known.* Coral snakes both lacking most red rings and having inordinately wide and very bright red rings have been found. *On the Florida Keys this species often lacks most of the yellow coloration.* Albinism has also been recorded. The smooth scales are in 15 rows, and the anal plate is divided, but if you are close enough to a live eastern coral snake to ascertain either of these facts and are not a trained herpetologist, you are far too close to this snake.

**Behavior** This fast-moving, burrowing snake is nervous, almost twitchy, when it is above ground. It then reacts very quickly to any molestation. When under suitable cover, it is usually much quieter and may remain in place for several days. For example, we visited one that we observed beneath a piece of plywood at the edge of our yard every day for almost a week before it disappeared. Conversely, another exploded from its resting area when the board beneath which it was hiding was lifted, disappeared into the surrounding leaves, and was never seen again. Coral snakes may be encountered both in rural and city settings. They are sometimes induced to move above ground by heavy rains that flood their burrows. Most surface-active eastern coral snakes that we have seen have been prowling amidst fallen leaves or pine needles during the daylight hours. Never prod or touch this snake.

**Habitat/Range** The eastern coral snake occurs in open woodlands, hammocks, and fields—even suburban backyards. It is seldom encountered only because the species is secretive, not because it is rare. This coral snake often hides under fallen tree trunks, beneath human-generated litter, in mats of vegetation, or even beneath the recumbent stems of lawn grasses. You would be amazed at how little cover is necessary to offer this snake an almost complete camouflage.

Outside of Florida, the eastern coral snake ranges along the Gulf and Atlantic coastal plains from eastern Louisiana to southeastern North Carolina. A disjunct population exists in interior Alabama.

**Abundance** This is a common snake throughout most of its Florida range. Because it is so secretive, populations persist even in city parks and suburban yards, agricultural areas, and wildlands.

**Prey** The coral snake preys principally on other snakes. Lizards such as glass lizards and skinks are also eaten.

**Reproduction** The eastern coral snake is oviparous. A normal clutch contains between 3 and 7 eggs. Up to 13 eggs in a clutch have been recorded. The babies have a full load of venom and are capable of biting at hatching.

**Similar snakes** No other ringed snake in Florida has the two caution colors— red and yellow—touching. However, be very cautious of gaudily ringed snakes in the Florida Keys. There the eastern coral snake often lacks much of the yellow.


## Vipers and Pit Vipers, Family Viperidae

This family of dangerously venomous front-fanged snakes contains two subfamilies, Viperinae (true vipers) and Crotalinae (pit vipers). Only the latter subfamily—which contains the copperheads, rattlesnakes, lanceheads, and their allies—is represented in the United States. In Florida, we have a copperhead, a cottonmouth, and three species of rattlesnakes.

Tales have filtered down through time of the monstrous rattlesnakes and immense cottonmouths that have been found, and these tales have become entrenched as fact rather than fiction. The truth is, to any unsuspecting person suddenly confronted with the whirring rattle and coiled countenance of a rattlesnake or with a big cottonmouth swallowing a fish on a stringer, that snake is going to look *big*. And the chances are pretty good that the snake's size will increase with each telling of the adventure. Pretty soon a 4-foot-long rattler or cottonmouth has grown to 7 feet and a 6-footer to 10. Photos can be deceiving. A camera is a pretty easy gadget to fool. By having the picture taken with a small diameter lens and by holding the rattler (the big ones are always dead) at arm's length in front of you, a 5-footer will take on the perspective of a 10-footer. The camera doesn't know, and the handlers aren't telling.

Skins can also be deceiving. A skin can stretch two inches per foot, so a 5-foot snake suddenly measures almost 6 feet.

The greatest officially authenticated recorded size for a rattlesnake of the United States is for an eastern diamondback that measured an even 8 feet. For the cottonmouth, the record is held by the Florida subspecies and stands at 6 feet 2½ inches. To have seen either of these would have been a memorable occurrence for a herpetologist, for by today's standards, a 4-foot rattlesnake or cottonmouth *is* big and a 6-footer of either is *huge*. Size exaggerations are excusable though, for most crotaline snakes are so heavy-bodied that they always look bigger than they actually are.

The term pit viper has been derived from the deep heat-sensory pit on each side of the face. So sensitive are these facial pits that by correcting for almost infinitesimally different temperatures registering in each pit, a pit viper can strike prey or predator in complete darkness.

The pit vipers have a long hollow fang attached to a moveable maxillary bone on each side of the upper jaw. The maxilla can be rotated posteriorly to fold the fangs against the roof of the mouth when the mouth is closed, or rotated anteriorly to direct the fangs almost straight forward for a gaping, lunging forward strike. If a fang breaks, it is quickly replaced.

The fangs are ducted to venom glands at the rear of the head. It is these glands, and the controlling muscles that surround them, that cause the posterior enlargement so typical of the head of the viperine snakes. A pit viper can regulate the amount of venom expended during a bite. Many bites are "dry";

no venom is injected during the strike. During other bites, a full complement of venom can be injected. Secondary infections can be caused by any bite.

The venom—a complex combination of proteins and enzymes—has been developed primarily for food procurement and secondarily as a defense mechanism. The drop-for-drop toxicity of pit viper venom varies species by species, and even within a species.

All crotalines have vertically elliptical pupils.

Although comparatively few humans are bitten by venomous snakes in Florida, pets are less fortunate. Dogs, especially, are frequently bitten, and bites to canines by pygmy rattlesnakes are commonplace. Treatment consists largely of steroids and antibiotics, with antivenin being used only when necessary.

**Crotaline husbandry** A state permit is required to keep any venomous snake in Florida. All require special knowledge to be handled safely. These snakes are best left unmolested in the field. If you are permitted and qualified to keep crotalines, always treat these snakes with the utmost respect. Never consider any tame. Handle them only with snake hooks or tongs. *Never* pin them with a hook behind the head and then grasp them. This not only can seriously injure the snake but also can easily open the way to your being bitten. Their cage should always be securely locked (see state regulations).

Despite the moccasins and the rattlesnakes having very different habitats and habits in the wild, these diverse snakes will do well in captivity when provided with a cage that is of moderate to large size. The cage requires only a dry, easily cleaned substrate, a hide box, and a water dish. Although some examples remain "testy," many crotalines adapt well to captivity. Some become so quiet that they allow their keeper to develop a false sense of security when working with them. Always remember that these are potentially deadly snakes with a lightning-fast strike and potent venom.

Copperheads can be picky eaters—especially if collected in the autumn, immediately prior to hibernation. It may be necessary to experiment to find the food item they like the best. Copperheads may eat insects (cicadas), frogs, toads, lizards, birds, or rodents. Eventually most can be induced to eat mice. Pygmy rattlesnakes and cottonmouths also have a varied diet, but they are usually less reluctant to eat. The typical rattlesnakes will usually readily accept rodents. Room temperatures of 75–85°F are satisfactory. A "hot spot" a few degrees warmer, created by an overhead bulb, should be provided.

## Copperheads and Cottonmouths, Genus *Agkistrodon*

All species in this genus should be considered dangerously venomous. In the United States, the members of this genus are colloquially referred to as moccasins, with the copperheads being highland moccasins and the cottonmouths being water moccasins. Moccasins, wherever found, are usually unceremoniously killed. Because the term *moccasin* has been broadened to encompass many of the harmless water snakes, we urge that it not be used.

Actually, the terms *copperhead* and *cottonmouth* are quite descriptive. The copperheads not only have a coppery-colored to russet head, but their banding is of a similar color. You have only to see the cottony-white gape of a frightened, defensive cottonmouth to understand the derivation of that name.

These snakes accept both endothermic (warm-blooded) and ectothermic (cold-blooded) prey. Prey items may vary from grasshoppers and cicadas to ground-dwelling birds and small mammals.

These snakes have a single row of subcaudal scales and no rattles. Despite lacking a rattle, by vibrating its tail in dried vegetation, a nervous copperhead or cottonmouth can produce a very audible whirring sound. The pupil is vertically elliptical.

Copperheads and cottonmouths birth live young. Studies have shown that copperheads may produce young only every second or third year—at least in the northern United States. Reproductive studies of cottonmouths are notably lacking, but it is speculated that cottonmouths from more northerly regions also breed biennially.

The young of all copperheads and cottonmouths have contrastingly colored (usually yellowish) tail tips they use for caudal luring (the adults of some races of copperhead retain the contrasting tail color throughout their lives). Caudal luring is an interesting manner of prey procurement. The snake coils, positions its tail rather near its head, elevates the tail, and rhythmically writhes the tail to and fro. Supposedly a frog or lizard mistakes the tail for a succulent insect, approaches to investigate, and is seized by the snake. As far as is known, only species (both harmless and venomous) with contrasting tail colors indulge in this behavior.

Two species—a copperhead and a cottonmouth (the latter with both a pure and an intergrade form)—occur in Florida.

These snakes have vertically elliptical pupils.

Cottonmouths are associated with aquatic habitats; copperheads with damp woodland or unkempt agricultural areas.

## 80. Southern Copperhead
*Agkistrodon contortrix contortrix*

**Dangerously Venomous** Despite having a less virulent venom than many other of the pit vipers, envenomation by a copperhead is not a pleasant experience. However, unless you are inordinately sensitive to the venom components, a bite is not usually considered life-threatening.

**Size** Copperheads are of moderately heavy girth. Most adult southern copperheads are between 26 and 34 inches in length. Occasional specimens may exceed 4 feet. Neonates average about 8¾ inches in length.

**Identification** The body scales of the southern copperhead are weakly keeled, and the subcaudal scales are either entirely in a single row or undivided anteriorly and divided posteriorly. The anal plate is undivided. The head is distinctly broader than the neck but is usually not triangular. The top of the head is seldom much darker than the face. A thin dark line runs from the snout, through the eye, to the back of the head.

The ground color of the southern copperhead is variable. It is usually tan or light brown. The dark, hourglass-shaped crossbands of this race of copperhead are often broken and offset at midline. Dark ventrolateral spots are present at regular intervals along the body and encroach on the outer edges of the ventral scutes. Typically, the belly is lighter than the dorsum and is variably smudged with dark pigment.

Neonates are paler than the adults and have a yellow to greenish-yellow tail tip.

**Behavior** Because they often remain quietly coiled, depending entirely on their camouflage color to avoid detection, copperheads can pose a hazard when near human habitations. As might be expected, when stepped on or otherwise jostled, the frightened snake will bite. Once riled, copperheads may strike rapidly and forcefully.

This is very much a wait-and-ambush predator, and a copperhead may remain virtually in the same spot for days or even weeks.

Although essentially diurnal during cool weather, the hot nights of summer—especially when accompanied by a gentle warm rain—will induce extensive nocturnal activity.

Although they can climb, copperheads are essentially terrestrial.

**Habitat/Range** In Florida, southern copperheads occur in the open woodlands surrounding wet-bottomed ravines. They may also be found in woodland clearings, at swamp edges, and near beaver ponds. The remarkable camouflage coloration of this snake assures that most copperheads, if quietly coiled in dead leaves and grasses, will be overlooked. If in areas of human activity, the coiled snakes may be easily stepped on. The latter often results in snakebite.

This snake will often conceal itself beneath manmade debris and seems particularly partial to discarded roofing tins and pieces of plywood.

Although the range of the southern copperhead comes virtually to the Florida state line over much of western Alabama, it is known to occur in Florida only in Escambia, Gadsden, Liberty, and Santa Rosa Counties.

**Abundance** This does not seem to be a particularly common snake in Florida, but neither, within its limited range in that state, is it rare. Elsewhere in its range (southeastern North Carolina to southeastern Missouri and eastern Texas) it can be an abundant species.

**Prey** Accepted prey items vary from cicadas and caterpillars, to lizards and amphibians, to small snakes, birds, and rodents.

**Reproduction** The southern copperhead is a live-bearing snake. The babies are birthed in a transparent, membranous sac from which they break free after only a few minutes. Clutches contain from 3 to 9 young.

**Similar snakes** Brightly patterned juvenile cottonmouths are often mistaken for copperheads. However, the cottonmouth has a broad dark eye stripe and brighter bands than the southern copperhead. Brown water snakes have heavily keeled scales and squared dorsal blotches that are separated from the squared lateral blotches. Milk snakes have narrow heads and squared dorsal blotches that are separated from small, often rounded lateral blotches. Hognosed snakes have an enlarged, pointed, and upturned rostral (nose) scale.

## 81. Florida Cottonmouth
*Agkistrodon piscivorous conanti*

**Dangerously Venomous** This snake has venom that is, drop-for-drop, more toxic than that of the related copperhead. Too, because of the snake's larger head (and size), more venom can be discharged during a bite. Also, because the cottonmouth is an inveterate scavenger, dangerous bacteria are usually introduced with each bite. Secondary infections may become of more concern that the actual envenomation.

A cottonmouth can deliver a venomous bite whether on land or submerged in water. Always give this interesting snake a wide berth.

**Size** The Florida cottonmouth is marginally, the largest of the three cottonmouth races. An adult size of 30 to 36 inches is commonly seen today. Although 5-footers were not uncommon in the 1970s, they are now a rarity. The record size is 74½ inches. Neonates average about 11½ inches in length.

**Identification** This is one of many Florida snakes—but the only venomous Florida species—to undergo dramatic ontogenetic (age-related) changes in color and pattern. Adults Florida cottonmouths are heavy-bodied and dark—olive-black to black—in color. Usually the only readily visible pattern is on the face. If the snake is wet, or freshly shed, traces of a body pattern may be discernible. If present, the pattern will be strongest on the lower sides. The facial pattern involves a broad, dark eyestripe, bordered above and below by light pigment, tan upper labials, and a brown-and-white marked lower jaw.

Neonates and juveniles are very brightly colored and strongly patterned, with the neonates being the brightest. Then, the eyestripe is very well defined, the top of the head is a rich-brown to almost russet, and irregular edged light and medium-dark brown bands (sometimes separated by even darker bands of brown to brownish-black) are present along the entire body. The tail tip is greenish-yellow. Well-defined darker spots may be present in some of the body bands. The upper lip is often orangish.

With age and growth, a suffusion of melanin darkens the body (including the tail tip) until the almost unicolored hue of the adult is attained. As with all cottonmouths, the 25 rows of scales are keeled, the anal plate entire, and the subcaudals undivided, at least anteriorly.

**Behavior** The Florida cottonmouth is, for a snake, often quite bold in its actions. They may crawl slowly away when approached or they may hold their ground. The slow departure is very unlike the headlong dash to safety indulged in by the *nonvenomous* water snakes. Whether coiled or stretched out, the cottonmouth usually holds its head tilted upward. Again, this is a very different posture than the straight-ahead head position of the nonvenomous water snakes. Although the cottonmouth is entirely capable of completely submerging, when unfrightened, a swimming cottonmouth sculls slowly away, head held well above the water, entire body on the surface. And once more, this is very different from the frenzied departure followed by immediate submersion of a harmless water snake. Often when a coiled cottonmouth is approached, it will remain in position, tilt its nose upward even more than normal, and gape widely, displaying the cottony-white interior of its mouth. A harmless snake *never* does that.

If a human happens to frighten a resting cottonmouth into motion by walking between it and its home water, the snake will often come straight toward them in an attempt to get to the water. Harmless water snakes *may* do this, but more often make a wide circle toward the water in an attempt to avoid the human. When near the human interloper, the cottonmouth may continue into the water or the snake may stop and gape. Either way, give it room.

Unlike most other Florida snakes, you may encounter a cottonmouth that will stand its ground or may actually come toward you. Remembering at that time that as the adage states, discretion *is* the better part of valor; retreat.

**Habitat/Range** This southeasternmost race of the cottonmouth is restricted in distribution almost entirely to Florida. It occurs throughout the state except in the western panhandle, where intergrades between it and the eastern cottonmouth are found. The Florida cottonmouth is also found in extreme southeastern and extreme southwestern Georgia. This big snake is associated with water, be it fresh, brackish, or (more rarely) salt, and whether the water is still or flowing. Expect it at stream- and river-side, in salt marshes, in tidally influenced estuaries, or resting on fallen tree trunks in woodland ponds. In other words, expect to see a cottonmouth whenever you are near water.

**Abundance** Although over the last few decades Florida cottonmouths have diminished noticeably in numbers and average adult size, this snake is still common throughout much of its range.

**Prey** This snake has truly catholic feeding habits. Prey may be alive or dead,

fresh or decomposing. Prey includes, but is not limited to, fish, frogs, salamanders, lizards, other snakes, small turtles, small mammals, and small birds.
Many cottonmouths are killed by vehicles as the snakes try to eat already dead
animals from busy roadways. Even gar carcasses, thrown away by many Florida fishermen, are eaten when found.

**Reproduction** From 3 to 12 babies seems the normal clutch size for this race.

**Similar snakes** Please see the next account for identification of the intergrade
cottonmouth of Florida's western panhandle. The southern copperhead lacks
a bold facial pattern. It is with the brown and the banded water snakes that the
Florida cottonmouth is most often confused. Please see the respective accounts for these harmless snakes beginning on pages 87 and 89. Compare the
pictures carefully. All harmless water snakes have round pupils, lack facial
pits, and almost never stand their ground if surprised.

### Cottonmouth Intergrades in Florida

### 82. Eastern Cottonmouth x Florida Cottonmouth
### *Agkistrodon piscivorous piscivorous* x *A. p. conanti*

On the western panhandle one will encounter cottonmouths that are intergrades between the Eastern and the Florida Cottonmouth, *Agkistrodon
piscivorous piscivorous* x *A. p. conanti*. As an intergrade (one that results from the breeding of one
subspecies with a second contiguous subspecies),
these snakes may resemble either of the parent
species more than the other, or be of intermediate
appearance. Usually these snakes in Florida look
much like the Florida cottonmouth, but may have less vivid facial markings
and be a little more on the olive side of black. They also may retain a little
more banding into adulthood. The body pattern will be strongest on the
lower sides. The facial pattern, which may be vague, involves a broad eye
stripe that is darker than the rest of the face and is bordered above and below
by light pigment. The upper labials (lip scales) are tan or olive and the lower
labials are pale brown, and the lower jaw is marked with olive and white.

Neonates and juveniles are very brightly colored and strongly patterned.
Their eye stripe is very well defined, the top of the head is a rich-brown to

almost russet, and irregular edged light and medium-dark brown bands (sometimes separated by even darker bands of brown to brownish-black) are present along the entire body. The tailtip is greenish-yellow. Well-defined darker spots may be present in some of the body bands. The upper lip may be orangish, light brown, or olive-brown. In Florida this intergrade form occurs only in the western panhandle.

## Rattlesnakes (Genus *Crotalus*)

The genus *Crotalus* is restricted to the New World. The various species occur from the southernmost of the western Canadian Provinces in the west and central New Hampshire in the east, southward through South America to Argentina. In the United States the genus is best represented west of the Mississippi River. East of the Mississippi, only two species occur, the timber rattlesnake and the eastern diamondbacked rattlesnake. These are both found in Florida.

The rattlesnakes of the genus *Crotalus* have finely fragmented crown scales. This alone will allow easy differentiation from the rattlers in the genus *Sistrurus* (the pygmy rattlers and massasaugas) which, like most harmless snakes, have 9 large plates on the top of their head.

Rattlesnakes are wait and ambush hunters that, by chemosensory testing, are able to unerringly position themselves along active rodent trails. Most strike and immediately release their prey, allowing the venom a chance to immobilize the stricken animal before trailing it. It has been shown that rattlesnakes are able to differentiate between the trail of a non-envenomated animal and an envenomated one, even if of the same species.

Prairies, open woodlands and their environs, sandy scrub, and other such areas are the habitats of rattlesnakes. In rural areas these snakes may occasionally be found in vacant lots and debris-filled yards.

## 83. Eastern Diamond-backed Rattlesnake
### *Crotalus adamanteus*

**Venomous** A full envenomation by a large example of this rattlesnake is life-threatening. Some will coil and begin rattling at the slightest provocation while others may never make a sound, even if prodded. Disposition is equally disparate. Some diamondbacks will strike wildly at any nearby movement while others will allow themselves to be lifted with a snakehook without showing any signs of bad temper.

**Size** Forty-two to 54 inches is the size typically seen today. A few decades ago 6-foot long individuals were not uncommon. The record size is an even 8 feet. Neonates average 13½ inches in length.

**Identification** This snake is normally an interesting and attractive combination of gray on gray with black and white highlights. Occasionally the ground color may be olive-brown. The white outlined black dorsal diamonds (with light centers) are characteristic. So too are the two diagonal white lines on each side of the face. The keeled scales are in 27 or 29 rows. The tail is paler and less prominently patterned than the anterior.

Neonates are similar in pattern to, but paler in coloration than, the adults.

**Behavior** Should you round a palmetto bush while walking through a Florida woodland and encounter one of these big snakes, it will be a memorable experience. Truthfully though, diamondbacks blend so well with their background that you (and we) probably walk by many and never even suspect their presence. Give a diamondback a background of a few fallen twigs, a patch of fallen dead leaves or pine needles, and a few blades of wiregrass and the rattler—even a big rattler—will literally disappear from sight. Although this remarkable camouflage stands the rattler in good stead, it can be very detrimental to the hiker who, entirely by accident, approaches too closely.

Although they seldom do, diamondbacks can climb, and they swim well. When in the water they generally hold both head and rattle elevated away from the water surface.

In Florida, diamondbacks seem to be primarily diurnal. In our many years of field observations we have found only two examples active after dark.

**Habitat/Range** This magnificent, but potentially deadly (and always dangerous) snake typifies the rural Florida of bygone decades. These are snakes of pineywoods and of the Everglades—of offshore Keys and of sandland hammocks—of palmetto scrublands and of coastal strand. In short, the eastern diamondback is able to utilize a wide variety of habitats, and which give ground only grudgingly to development and its concurrent habitat fragmentation.

This, the largest known rattlesnake of the United States, ranges throughout Florida and its Keys. Beyond Florida it is a coastal plain creature of suitable habitats from central North Carolina to eastern Louisiana.

**Abundance** Although it is still found generally over the entire state, there are far fewer diamond-backed rattlesnakes today than only 10 or 20 years ago. While the loss of habitats to development and the fragmentation by roads of remaining habitats has certainly played a pert in the population reductions of this snake, so, too, have collection for both the pet trade and the skin trade, and the cyclic decline of the diamondback's primary prey—rabbits. Today (2001) rabbits seem to be on the increase again. It will be interesting to note whether populations of diamondbacks rebound noticeably.

**Prey** This large rattlesnake eats all manner of mammals, but cottontails and marsh rabbits are its most important foods. Newly born diamondbacks are large enough to eat adult mice or newborn rabbits.

**Reproduction** Female eastern diamondbacks do not grow rapidly, even in times of plenty. Since size as well as age plays important parts in their reproductive biology, diamondbacks are often several years old before they first breed. Females may breed annually, but more often produce young only biennially or triennially. Parturition occurs in mid- to late summer. Clutch size varies from 3 to 20 (rarely a few more, commonly 6 to 10).

**Similar species** No other Florida snake has the dorsal diamond-pattern and rattle. There are no similar species.

## 84. Timber Rattlesnake (Canebrake phase)
### *Crotalus horridus* (*atricaudatus*)

**Venomous** This large and potentially dangerous rattlesnake is of very variable disposition. Some coil and begin rattling while a provoking object is still some distance away. Others may, if startled while moving, stop moving but remain stretched fully out, remaining silent, or they may rattle furiously. Many make a frenzied dash for safety with the rattle buzzing sporadically. Still others will lie quietly until they are actually jostled, then either attempt a dashing, headlong escape or quickly strike, either with or without rattling.

The venom is geographically variable, being predominantly hemolytic throughout much of the range, but is highly neurotoxic and very dangerously potent in the Florida population.

**Size** This southern phase of the timber rattlesnake is adult at from 44 to 54 inches in length, and rather regularly attains 60 inches. The largest specimens slightly exceed 72 inches. Neonates average 13½ inches in length.

**Identification** Whether this rattlesnake is a subspecies, *Crotalus horridus atricaudatus* (as was long thought), or a color phase—actually there's not much difference between the two—remains arguable. Although we would prefer to think of it as a subspecies, the current taxonomic bent is to group it with the more northerly timber rattlesnake and make no nomenclatural differentiation.

The scales of the canebrake rattlesnake are arranged in from 21 to 25 rows, with the norm being 25. There are 21 to 29 dark bands, usually in the form on anteriorly directed chevrons, on the body. In Florida the body color may vary from yellowish-gray, through pale brown, to buff. The posterior third or quarter of the body becomes increasingly suffused with black pigment until the posterior one fifth of the body and the tail are so dark that a pattern is difficult to discern. The coloration of the belly is quite like the dorsal ground color, but is variably stippled with dark pigment.

A broad, dark, band angles downward from the eye to and past the back of the mouth. This remains easily visible throughout life on both sexes. A broad, rust-colored vertebral stripe that is strongest anteriorly, fades measurably posteriorly, but usually remains visible until obscured by the black pigment of the rear of the body.

Neonates are similar in pattern to, but paler in coloration than, the adults. The ground coloration of baby canebrakes is often a rather light gray.

**Behavior** Although these primarily terrestrial snakes can climb, they do so rather infrequently. They are also quite capable of swimming. This is a retiring and easily overlooked rattlesnake species. Despite being killed on sight, canebrake rattlesnakes seem to persist in areas of human habitation much more successfully than the diamondback. In one farming area of north central Florida canebrakes can be seen crossing roads in the evening with some regularity, but are very difficult to find during the hours of daylight, even when a concerted search for them is made.

Canebrake rattlers blend easily and well with even just a little background debris. A few fallen leaves, a stick or two, and a patch of dark soil will render a

coiled 4-foot long canebrake virtually invisible. These snakes may coil beneath woodland leaf litter, showing only the tip of the nose and the eyes.

**Habitat/Range** Although canebrake rattlers stray (usually fatally for them)
into nearby yards and parking lots, they are traditionally a snake of Florida's
wooded lowlands and seem to especially favor the non-flooded environs of
rivers, swamps, and riparian corridors.

As traditionally defined, the range of the canebrake rattlesnake extends
southward along the coastal plain and eastern Piedmont from southeastern
Virginia to north central Florida, then westward to central Texas. This race
extends its range northward in the Mississippi Valley to southern Illinois.

**Abundance** Populations of this snake persist, sometimes in fair numbers, in
the farming communities, wooded parks, and preserves, of north central
Florida.

**Prey** The canebrake rattlesnake eats all manner of rodents, lagomorphs, and
ground-dwelling birds. Newly born canebrake rattlesnakes are large enough
to eat nearly adult mice. They may more rarely accept amphibians and lizards.

**Reproduction** In Florida most female canebrake rattlers begin breeding in
their fourth or fifth year of life. Parturition occurs in mid- to late summer.
Clutch size varies from 3 to 19, with between 6 and 10 being the usual number
of babies produced. A female may produce young annually, biennially, or at
even longer intervals.

**Similar snakes** The pattern of dorsal chevrons and the rattle make this an
unmistakable snake in Florida.

## Pygmy Rattlesnakes and Massasaugas (Genus *Sistrurus*)

Only two of the three species currently contained in this genus occur in the
United States. Each species is divided into three subspecies. Only one subspecies of one species occurs in Florida.

The members of the genus *Sistrurus* are small, easily excitable, rattlesnakes
with slender tails and proportionately small rattles. The whirring, warning,
rattle of even an enraged snake can be difficult for a human to hear.

Although the drop for drop potency of the venom of these rattlesnakes is
quite high, the fangs of the snakes are relatively short and the venom yield
proportionately low.

The presence of the 9 unfragmented crown scales differentiates the pygmy rattlers and the massasaugas from the eastern members of the typical rattle-snakes (genus *Crotalus*), which have thoroughly fragmented crown scales.

The scales are keeled, the anal plate and subcaudal scales are undivided, and the pupil is vertically elliptical. The head is distinctly larger than the neck, but not overly broad.

In suitable habitat in Florida, the dusky pygmy rattlesnake can be present in such immense numbers that these might even be termed concentrations. The young of the pygmy rattlesnakes have yellowish tailtips which are used in caudal luring of prey.

Prairies, canal-edges, and open but damp woodlands are among the habitats utilized by this little snake.

## 85. Dusky Pygmy Rattlesnake
### *Sistrurus miliarius barbouri*

**Dangerously Venomous** Although quite potent in drop for drop toxicity, the small size of this rattler and the correspondingly low venom yield allow most bites sustained by an otherwise healthy adult to be considered non-life-threatening.

**Size** The dusky pygmy rattlesnake is adult at from 14 to 20 inches in length and has a verified record size of only 31.5 inches. Neonates are a slender 6.25 inches (average) in length.

**Identification** This is a dark, yet prominently patterned little rattlesnake. The ground color of most specimens is of some shade (usually dark) of gray. There is a row of prominent black dorsal blotches as well as a row of lateral blotches on each side. An orange vertebral stripe is usually present (at least anteriorly) between the dark dorsal blotches. The lateral blotches are well separated from the row of dorsal blotches. An elongate pair of dark blotches run from above the eyes to the anterior nape and a dark ocular stripe extends from each eye to the rear of the head. The venter is usually lighter than the dorsum and bears paired, but variably shaped, dark blotches.

Neonates are usually more intensely colored and patterned than the adults and have a yellowish-green tailtip.

**Behavior** This little rattlesnake varies widely in temperament, but many examples are nervous and irritable. Others are quiet—even laid back—in attitude. At best, the tiny rattle produces hardly more than a low buzz, hence is often unheard and unheeded.

When alerted, prior to striking, pygmy rattlers will often coil rather loosely, face their perceived adversary, and twitch their head nervously.

**Habitat/Range** The dusky pygmy rattlesnake ranges along the coastal plains from southeastern South Carolina to western Alabama. It is found throughout Florida. This snake may be found in a wide spectrum of habitats. These vary from pinewoods/scrub oak regions to open, mixed, woodlands. It is common on wet prairies, near the environs of marshes, at swamp edges, on road verges that parallel drainage canals, and near agricultural areas. It often thrives in suburban and rural areas replete with yard litter, along the edges of dumps, and may be seen crossing roadways on warm evenings.

**Abundance** Three words say it all about this snake—"common to abundant."

**Prey** Frogs, lizards, and mice are the preferred prey items of this little snake. The nestlings of ground-nesting bird species are more rarely taken.

**Reproduction** Clutches of up to two dozen (rarely more) babies are produced annually. The neonates are born from mid- to late-summer.

**Similar snakes** This is the only small rattlesnake with large crown scales in Florida.

# Introduced Venomous Snakes

Despite a cobra or other venomous snake species occasionally being caught in Florida, there is no evidence that any dangerous snake is yet established in the state.

# Peripheral Venomous Snakes

Of the North American venomous snake species, only the western cottonmouth is a form peripheral to Florida. This race of the cottonmouth ranges eastward to the Alabama-Florida state line, at the far western border of the panhandle. Some cottonmouths found in Escambia County, Florida, look very much like the western race in appearance but are probably of intergrade status genetically.

## 86. Western Cottonmouth
### *Agkistrodon piscivorous leucostoma*

This snake is a dangerously venomous, always defensive, and sometimes moderately aggressive serpent. Always give this interesting snake a wide berth.

The smallest of the three races of cottonmouths, this snake is adult at between 26 and 40 inches; seldom is a length of 48 inches exceeded. However, the record size is 62 inches. This race is the darkest of the cottonmouths and has the most obscure pattern. The facial pattern *may be* fairly well defined but is often quite indistinct. The dorsal coloration is usually dusky black. If markings are visible, they will be most prominent laterally. The belly is tan to brown smudged with black. The supralabial (upper lip) scales are usually lighter than the face, being tan or olive. Light markings can usually be seen on the lower labial scales. Neonates are very brightly colored and strongly patterned. Their eye-stripe is very well defined, the top of the head is brown and irregularly edged light and medium-dark brown bands (sometimes separated by even darker bands of brown to brownish-black) are present along the entire body. The tail tip is greenish-yellow. Darker spots may be present in some of the body bands. The upper lip may be light brown or olive-brown. This snake occurs from near the Alabama-Florida state line westward to central Texas and southern Illinois.

# Glossary

**Aestivation** A period of warm weather inactivity; often triggered by excessive heat or drought.

**Albino** Lacking black pigment.

**Amelanistic** Reptilian equivalent of albinism.

**Anerythristic** Lacking red pigment.

**Anterior** Toward the front.

**Anus** The external opening of the cloaca; the vent.

**Aposematic** With bright flash colors.

**Arboreal** Tree-dwelling.

**Autotomize** The ability to cast off the tail.

**Boid/Boidae** Boas and pythons.

**Brille** The transparent scale that covers the snake's eye.

**Brumation** Often used to describe reptilian and amphibian hibernation.

**Canthus** The ridge on the top of the snout.

**Caudal** Pertaining to the tail.

**Cloaca** The common chamber into which digestive, urinary, and reproductive systems empty and which itself opens exteriorly through the vent or anus.

**Colubrine/Colubridae** The largest of the snake groupings, containing such snakes as racers, garters, rats, kings, and gophers.

**Congeneric** Contained in the same genus.

**Conspecific** A snake (often a subspecies) of the same species.

**Constricting** To wrap tightly in coils and squeeze.

**Crepuscular** Active at dusk and/or dawn.

**Deposition** As used here, the laying of the eggs or birthing of young.

**Deposition site** The spot chosen by the female to lay her eggs or have young.

**Dimorphic** A difference in form, build, or coloration involving the same species; often sex-linked.

**Diurnal** Active in the daytime.

**Dorsal** Pertaining to the back; upper surface.

**Dorsolateral** Pertaining to the upper sides.

**Dorsum** The upper surface.

**Ecdysis** The shedding of the skin.

**Ectothermic** Cold-blooded; having a temperature regulated by the environment.

**Endemic** Restricted to a certain (usually geographic) area.

**Endothermic** Warm-blooded; being able to maintain one's body temperature without an external heat source.

**Erythristic** A prevalence of red pigment.

**Extralimital** Outside of a given range.

**Form** An identifiable species or subspecies.

**Fossorial** Adapted for burrowing. A burrowing species.

**Genus** A taxonomic classification of a group of species having similar characteristics. The genus falls between the next higher designation of *family* and the next lower designation of *species*. Genera is the plural of genus. The genus is always capitalized.

**Glottis** The opening of the windpipe.

**Heliothermic** Pertaining to a species that basks in the sun to thermoregulate.

**Hemipenes** The dual copulatory organs of male lizards and snakes.

**Herpetoculture** The captive breeding of reptiles and amphibians.

**Herpetologist** One who engages in herpetology.

**Herpetology** The study (often scientifically oriented) of reptiles and amphibians.

**Hibernacula** Winter dens.

**Hybrid** Offspring resulting from the breeding of two species.

**Insular** As used here, island-dwelling.

**Intergrade** Offspring resulting from the breeding of two subspecies.

**Interstitial** The skin between the scales.

**Jacobson's organs** Highly innervated olfactory pits in the palate of snakes and lizards.

**Juvenile** A young or immature specimen.

**Keel** A ridge (along the center of a scale).

**Labial** Pertaining to the lips.

**Lateral** Pertaining to the side.

**Melanism** A profusion of black pigment.

**Mental** The scale at the tip of the lower lip.

**Middorsal** Pertaining to the middle of the back.

**Midventral** Pertaining to the center of the belly or abdomen.

**Migration** As used here, a mass movement (often unidirectional) by snakes.

**Monotypic** Containing only one type.

**Natricine/Natricinae** A member of the subfamily containing garter, water, brown, and related colubrine snakes.

**Nocturnal** Active at night.

**Ocelli** Circular markings.

**Ontogenetic** Age-related (color) changes.

**Ophiophagous** Feeding on snakes.

**Oviparous** Reproducing by means of eggs that hatch after laying.

**Ovoviviparous** Reproducing by means of shelled or membrane- contained eggs that hatch prior to or at deposition.

**Photoperiod** The daily/seasonally variable length of the hours of daylight.

**Poikilothermic** A species with no internal body temperature regulation. The old term was *cold-blooded*.

**Postocular** To the rear of the eye.

**Prehensile** Adapted for grasping.

**Race** A subspecies.

**Rostral scale** The (often modified) scale on the tip of the snout.

**Rugose** Not smooth; wrinkled or tuberculate.

**Saxicolous** Rock-dwelling.

**Scute** Scale.

**Species** A group of similar creatures that produce viable young when breeding. The taxonomic designation that falls beneath *genus* and above *subspecies*. Abbreviated "sp."

**Subspecies** The subdivision of a species. A race that may differ slightly in color, size, scalation, or other criteria. Abbreviated "ssp."

**Supralabials** The upper lip scales.

**Sympatric** Occurring together.

**Taxonomy** The science of classification of plants and animals.

**Terrestrial** Land-dwelling.

**Thermoreceptive** Sensitive to heat.

**Thermoregulate** To regulate (body) temperature by choosing a warmer or cooler environment.

**Vent** The external opening of the cloaca; the anus.

**Venter** The underside of a creature; the belly.

**Ventral** Pertaining to the undersurface or belly.

**Ventrolateral** Pertaining to the sides of the venter, or belly.

# References

Abrahamson, W. G., and D. C. Hartnett. 1990. *Ecosystems of Florida.* Orlando: University of Central Florida Press.

Ashton, Ray E., Jr., and Patricia S. Ashton. 1981. *The snakes.* Pt. 1 of *Handbook of reptiles and amphibians of Florida.* Miami: Windward Press.

Bartlett, Richard D. 1988. *In search of reptiles and amphibians.* Leiden: E. J. Brill.

———. 1989. *Digest for the successful terrarium.* Morris Plains, N.J.: Tetra Press.

Behler, John L., and F. Wayne King. 1997. *The Audubon Society field guide to North American reptiles and amphibians.* New York: Alfred A. Knopf.

Blanchard, F. N. 1938. *Snakes of the genus* Tantilla *in the United States.* Field Museum of Natural History 20, no. 28: 369–76.

Blaney, R. M. Systematics of the common kingsnake, *Lampropetis getulus* (Linnaeus). *Tulane Zoological Studies* 19 (nos. 3–4): 47–103.

Burbrink, Frank T. 2001. *Systematics of the eastern ratsnake complex* (Elaphe Obsoleta). Herpetological Monographs, no. 15: 1–53.

Butler, J. A., T. W. Hull, and R. Franz. 1995. Neonate aggregations and maternal attendance of young in the eastern diamondback rattlesnake (*Crotalus adamanteus*). *Copeia* 1: 196–98.

Carr, Archie F., and Coleman J. Goin. 1959. *Guide to the reptiles, amphibians, and freshwater fishes of Florida.* Gainesville: University of Florida Press.

Conant, Roger. 1956. A review of two rare pine snakes from the Gulf coastal plain. *American Museum Novitates,* no. 1781: 17–21.

Conant, Roger, and Joseph T. Collins. 1998. *A field guide to reptiles and amphibians: Eastern and Central North America.* 3d ed., expanded. Boston: Houghton Mifflin.

Crother, Brian I., chair. 2000. Scientific and standard English names of amphibians and reptiles of North America north of Mexico, with comments regarding confidence in our understanding. Herpetological Circular no. 29. Society for the Study of Amphibians and Reptiles.

Dodd, C. K., Jr. 1992. Biological diversity of a temporary pond herpetofauna in North Florida sandhills. *Biodiversity and Conservation* 1: 125–42.

Dowling, Herndon G. 1950. *Studies of the black swamp snake* Seminatrix pygaea *(Cope), with descriptions of two new subspecies.* Ann Arbor, University of Michigan Press.

Dundee, Harold A., and Douglas A. Rossman. 1989. *The amphibians and reptiles of Louisiana.* Baton Rouge: Louisiana State University Press.

Ernst, Carl H. 1989. *Snakes of eastern North America.* Fairfax, Va.: George Mason University Press.

———. 1992. *Venomous reptiles of North America.* Washington, D.C.: Smithsonian Institution Press.

Franz, Richard. 1977. Observations on the food, feeding behavior, and parasites of the striped swamp snake, *Regina alleni. Herpetologica* 33: 91–94.

Gloyd, Howard K., and Roger Conant. 1990. *Snakes of the* Agkistrodon *complex.* Oxford, Ohio: Society for the Study of Amphibians and Reptiles.

Godley, J. S. 1980. *Foraging ecology of the striped swamp snake (*Regina alleni*) in southern Florida.* Ecological Monographs, no. 50: 411–36.

Greene, Harry W. 1997. *Snakes: The evolution of mystery in nature.* Berkeley: University of California Press.

Grobman, Arnold B. 1984. *Scutellation variation in* Opheodrys aestivus. Bulletin of the Florida State Museum of Biological Science 29: 153–70.

Grogan, W. L., Jr. 1974. Effects on accidental envenomation from saliva of the eastern hognose snake, *Heterodon platyrhinos. Herpetologica* 30: 248–49.

Haast, W. E., and R. Anderson. 1981. *Complete guide to the snakes of Florida.* Miami: Phoenix.

Harris, H. H. 1965. *Case reports on two dusky pygmy rattlesnake bites* (Sistrurus miliarius barbouri). Bulletin of the Maryland Herpetological Society, no. 2: 8–10.

Hayes, M.P. 1985. Food of the *Coluber constrictor priapus* (southern black racer). *Herpetological Review* 16: 78.

Holman, J. A., and W. H. Hill. 1961. A mass unidirectional movement of *Natrix sipedon pictiventris. Copeia* 1961: 498–99.

Jackson D. L., and R. Franz. 1981. Ecology of the eastern coral snake in northern peninsular Florida. *Herpetologica* 37: 213–28.

Lawler, Howard E. 1977. The status of *Drymarchon corais couperi* (Holbrook), the eastern indigo snake, in the southeastern United States. *Herpetological Review* 8: 76–79.

Mehrtens, John M. 1987. Living snakes of the world in color. New York: Sterling.

Meshaka, Walter E., Jr. 1994. Clutch parameters of *Storeria dekayi,* Holbrook (Serpentes Colubridae) from Southcentral Florida. *Brimleyana* 21: 73–76.

Moler, P. E., ed. 1992. *Amphibians and reptiles.* Vol. 3 of Rare and endangered biota of Florida. Gainesville: University Press of Florida.

Myers, Charles W. 1965. *Biology of the ringneck snake* (Diadophis punctatus) *in Florida.* Florida State Museum of Biological Science Bulletin, no. 10: 43–49.

Pisani, G. R., J. T. Collins, and S. R. Edwards. 1973. A re-evaluation of the subspecies of *Crotalus horridus.* Kansas Academy of Sciences 75, no. 3: 255–63.

Riemer, W. J. 1957. The snake *Farancia abacura:* An attended nest. *Herpetologica* 13: 31–32.

Rossi, John V. 1992. *Eastern area.* Vol. 1 of *Snakes of the United States and Canada: Keeping them healthy in captivity.* Melbourne, Fla.: Krieger.

Rossi, John V., and Roxanne Rossi. 1993. Notes on the captive maintenance and feeding behavior of a juvenile short-tailed snake (*Stilosoma extenuatum*). *Herpetological Review* 24, no. 3: 100–101.

———. 1995. *Western area.* Vol. 2 of *Snakes of the United States and Canada: Keeping them healthy in captivity.* Melbourne, Fla.: Krieger.

Teather, K. L. 1991. The relative importance of visual and chemical cues for foraging in newborn blue-striped garter snakes (*Thamnophis sirtalis similis*). *Behaviour* 117, no. 3–4: 225–61.

Timmerman, W. W. 1989. Home range, habitat use, and behavior of the eastern diamondback rattlesnake. Master's thesis, University of Florida.

Wharton, C. H. 1960. Birth and behavior of a brood of the cottonmouth, *Agkistrodon piscivorous leucostoma,* with notes on tail-luring. *Herpetologica* 16: 125–29.

Wright, Albert H., and A. A. Wright. 1957. *Handbook of snakes.* Vols. 1 & 2. Ithaca, N.Y.: Comstock.

# Index

# About the Authors

R. D. Bartlett is a herpetologist/herpetoculturist who has authored more than five hundred articles and four books and has co-authored an additional thirty books. He lectures extensively and has participated in field studies across North and Latin America. In 1970, he began the Reptilian Breeding and Research Institute (RBRI), a private facility. Since its inception, more than twenty species of reptiles and amphibians have been bred at RBRI, some for the first time in the United States under captive conditions. Successes at RBRI include several endangered species. Bartlett is a member of numerous herpetological and conservation organizations, was a co-host on an on-line reptile and amphibian forum, and is a contributing editor of the magazine *Reptiles*.

Patricia Bartlett is a biologist and historian who has authored eight books and co-authored thirty-one books. A museum administrator for the last fifteen years, she has worked in both history and science museums. She received the America Public Works Association Heritage Award in 1985 and serves in numerous local and state organizations.